Crowns of Beauty is a compelling story about one woman's courage in the face of seemingly insurmountable odds. A narrative filled with heartbreak and joy, Sophie's journey on the mission field is an incredible account of bravery and selflessness that will leave you wishing the story would never end. For every individual who has ever wondered if one person can make a difference, *Crowns of Beauty* serves as the ultimate example of world-changing faith.

–Russell Johnson
Lead Pastor
The Pursuit NW

In a world where finding real heroes outside of comic books and movies isn't easy, Sophie Hartman changes things. Her story is an example of a heart, young enough to be self consumed, finding a way to be ever listening to hear the call of God and respond with a "yes, Lord." She doesn't follow the normal paths of her generation or even what is genuinely expected for a young woman her age. She sees a need and her response is to help. She hears a cry and engages to soothe. She finds an orphan and becomes a mother. She shows off a beautiful God response to a precious and costly need. As an adoptive mother myself I choke back emotion knowing what that cost is and knowing also the reward it has, exposing me to light and drowning me in unconditional love. If everyone carried a Sophie Hartman heart, the world would have no orphans.

–Rita Springer
Recording Artist, Worship Leader, & Author of Finding Eve

Sophie Hartman's *Crowns of Beauty* proves yet again how the adventure of following God—including to remote Zambia—is so much more about what God wants to teach us than it is about what we hope to teach others. Anyone considering mission work, social justice, or international child welfare needs to read this book. Through *Crowns of Beauty* the reader will be privy to a young missionary's most vulnerable and harrowing moments on her journey, including her righteous anger toward unspeakable injustice, her fear and despair when all seems lost—and her tears of joy when the impossible suddenly becomes possible.

–Andrew Schneidler
Child Welfare Attorney and Founder of the Permanence Project

Have you ever wondered what it would mean if you fully and completely gave yourself over to God's calling in your life, everyday? Crowns of Beauty is one woman's story of faithfully listening, and obediently following God's voice - *everyday*. Sophie's journey will challenge you to invite the Holy Spirit into all parts of your life, from the significant to the mundane. As you travel with her through these stories let your heart be broken, filled and transformed. Be prepared to walk away with a changed heart!

–Cari Armbruster
Executive Director of Alliance for Children Everywhere

In *Crowns of Beauty*, Sophie Hartman strips away the glorified mission field and introduces us to the plight of the people and to the sounds, the smells, and the cries that permeate the air in Zambia. Meet Nakukenga, Mapalo, and Mutinta, just a few of the children who stole Sophie's heart and ignited a passion in her soul for this African nation. Sophie's words will take you to the roads where you will feel the grit on your skin and the dust in your teeth. This account of her mission work in Zambia, which began with a simple yes, will transform your heart for orphan care and will reveal God's passionate love for His people. Two decades her senior, I can only wonder what God would have done with my life had I approached His throne with such abandon! Read this book as soon as possible to join Sophie in serving a relentless God who loves you immensely and has great plans for you in the decades ahead.

–Rebecca Vahle
Executive Director of Family to Family Support Network
and Host of *Adoption Perspectives* Radio Show

Crowns of Beauty is the breathtaking story of one woman's fierce, faithful love for Jesus and of her calling to follow Him into the gritty brokenness and the disturbing injustices faced by orphans in sub-Saharan Africa.

Sophie humbly and transparently guides readers through dark, faith-testing valleys while also revealing the redemptive beauty of Christ's victorious pursuit of His "sought after" ones! *Crowns of Beauty* is a beautifully written reminder that God is faithful to bring joy amid suffering and light in the midst of darkness and that the breakthrough He provides often comes when we find ourselves in the hardest and most desperate places. But once it comes and fear is conquered, freedom in Christ rushes in as a raging river of life!

–Gary Schneider
Founder and President of Every Orphan's Hope

Crowns of Beauty is provocative, disturbing, and inspiring, a book that will challenge readers to move out of the safety of their churches. Sophie is a Spirit-led, God-driven, compassionate, courageous, and God-fearing woman, and she lives a life where love knows no bounds. We are missionaries who have been in Zambia for fifteen years, and our hearts swell with pride and love for Sophie as she loves and serves the beautiful women and children of Zambia.

–John and Susan Chalkias
Executive Director and Founder/Director of Operations
Seeds of Hope Children's Ministry

Be prepared. You are about to dive into a compelling story about the cost and the rewards of following Jesus, about looking fear in the eye and advancing resolutely forward. It's the narrative of someone who has been given a large measure of faith; while this gift leads Sophie into messy and painful places, it also sustains her. Sophie shares her excruciating but hope-filled account of discovering one of the keys to the kingdom: a life poured out in love.

Crowns of Beauty is not just about missionary adventures on foreign soil. It depicts several phases of discipleship we can all learn from—hearing God's voice, following His requests even when it costs us dearly, and understanding that lovers of His presence satisfy His heart much more than kingdom employees. This book will challenge your own journey with Jesus and will stir in you His compassion for the least and the lost around you. Africa has many physical orphans, but America has even more emotional and spiritual ones. I pray this story will activate your willingness to follow Jesus even if that means going into the dark, to learn to be loved by Him, and in turn, to discover the hidden treasures in the darkness, the riches stored in secret places—just as Sophie has.

–Bethany Arndt
Director and Founder of Baby Safe, South Africa

With each page, my heart was completely engrossed and undone by Sophie's story. I could not put the book down. Her words pierced my heart and gave me a greater understanding of Jesus's perfect love, compassion, and justice in the midst of our human brokenness. Sophie gently invites and challenges readers to have a deeper, more authentic relationship with our Savior. To me, that is the greatest gift one can offer the world.

–Grace Theisen
Cofounder of Songs Against Slavery

Crowns of Beauty is captivating and inspiring and will grip the hearts of all those who read it. This book is a cry for justice and will stir your heart for intercession and for greater intimacy with Papa God. It will challenge you and leave you with hope for tomorrow and with strength and faith to continue pressing on. *Crowns of Beauty* will remind you once again that God is always faithful and that He will carry you through, turning what was once broken into something beautiful.

–Jaclyn Miller
Founder and Director of Marked by Heaven

Crowns of Beauty is full of contradictions: heartbreaking and glorious, painful and healing, ugly and beautiful. Reading the details of a young woman's life on foreign soil, it is impossible not to be fully transported to the dust of the earth in that African land and to feel in your soul every crushing defeat and every joyous victory as she champions the least of these. The people Sophie introduces you to will stay with you long after the final page. She lends a voice to the voiceless, and they no longer live as unnamed, faceless women and children of poverty and injustice but rather as Espina,

Emmanuel, Mutinta, and countless more. Sophie honors their lives and their stories with profound grace and with captivating description.

–Jennifer Tompkins
Cofounder and President of Called to Love Ministry

This beautifully raw testimony has produced a stirring within my soul to see God more clearly, to experience Him more fully, and to love Him more deeply. The Holy Spirit is alive and evident in Sophie's life and writing, pointing to the magnificent and intimate heart of our King. These words will surely be a blessing to many.

–Amy Bardi
Founder and Executive Director of Clothed in Hope

CROWNS
of BEAUTY

*A Story of Brokenness, Courage and
Beauty Rising from Ashes*

SOPHIE HARTMAN

WESTBOW
PRESS®
A DIVISION OF THOMAS NELSON
& ZONDERVAN

WestBow Press books may be ordered through booksellers or by contacting:

WestBow Press
A Division of Thomas Nelson & Zondervan
1663 Liberty Drive
Bloomington, IN 47403
www.westbowpress.com
1 (866) 928-1240

ISBN: 978-1-5127-3928-2 (sc)
ISBN: 978-1-5127-3930-5 (hc)
ISBN: 978-1-5127-3929-9 (e)

Library of Congress Control Number: 2016906614

Print information available on the last page.

WestBow Press rev. date: 5/4/2016

CONTENTS

For You, my beautiful carpenter, my beloved bridegroom, the love of my life. Jesus, forever I will pour out my perfume at Your feet. Oh, to behold You.

And for those awaiting justice. Thank you, beautiful friends who suffer without ever losing hope, for teaching me so much about the heart, the intentions, and the character of Jesus. It would take years for me to explain all that I have learned from you and to recount all the ways I am indebted to you. The Bible tells us to prepare a feast for the one who cannot give back, and though the world assumes that you are the ones who cannot give back, we both know it is I who can never repay you. Thank you for preparing a table for me and for inviting me in. Thank you for living authentically before me and for teaching me that beauty isn't absent from brokenness. Thank you for giving me permission to embrace my own brokenness, that I might feel God reaching into the depths of my story and making me beautiful. I am eternally indebted to you.

And, of course, for you, my precious girls—Miah, my mighty oak, and Carmel, my harvest child. Thank you for making me a mama and for the grace you give me every day. I love you fiercely.

AUTHOR'S NOTE

Authoring your own story is no small task. In the last few years as I have given myself to writing and rewriting this account of my journey, I have discovered that this type of work truly demands great precision. What a challenge it is to bring forth such rich authenticity and integrity while keeping in mind that my perspective is just one in a sea of hundreds. I have done my best to accurately and equally portray my fear and confidence, my brokenness and courage, my independence and naiveté, while also making it a priority to honor those whose stories collide with mine. In every last word of this work, my intention has always been to honor those who have sacrificed to contribute to my life and to my legacy in the Lord.

Though many of the people involved in this story gladly consented to have their names and stories shared, I have decided to change all the names to protect identities. Outside of my name and my children's names, I have made only two exceptions, two little boys whose safety is of no concern because they are eternally wrapped in the arms of Jesus. I have also changed the names of several locations, though the entire story takes place in the incredible nation of Zambia.

I have carefully written the stories contained in these chapters with an absolute unwillingness to exploit the children to whom they belong. I have spent countless hours poring over each account, making sure that my sharing is not purposed for my own gain. I hope that through each story my voice will sound an alarm for all those willing to fight for justice, calling them to hear the Word of the Lord for the sake of the world.

With sobriety and deep gratitude,
Sophie Hartman

ACKNOWLEDGMENTS

For these, my closest confidants, whose lives have forever marked mine, any expression of gratitude seems far too small, but still I thank:

My beautiful daughters, Miah and Carmel: You two undo me. Thank you for always being such brave lovers and for letting me be your mama. You are without a doubt the greatest gifts I have ever been given. Your smiles make me come alive, and your tender hearts are the sweetest I've ever known. I love you all the way, my precious two.

Samantha Hartman: Thank you for your hard work in putting together pieces for this book. Your perspective has been invaluable and your poetic words have added a unique dynamic to this story. Thank you for the honesty and vulnerability that you have so willingly shared, and thank you for the privilege of watching you fall in love with Jesus and recognize your deep need for Him. Your life is a powerful testimony. I will always be proud of you.

Mom, Dad, Kyle (and Samantha): I love and honor you. I pray that through this work, another wave of Jesus's love will cover us all. I am so eager to see what He has in store for our family in the decades to come. You have my heart, and though we have walked through many painful seasons, I'm grateful to be yours.

Megan Malnar: I adore you. Thank you for your compassion, integrity, and vulnerability, and thank you for the way you have stood beside me through the writing of this book. Thank you for your friendship, which bears with me in all of my weakness, and for the purity of your commitment to me. You contend for my greatness in the Lord like no other, and for that, I am so grateful. We both know that our friendship is a miraculous gift from Jesus, and it will always leave a wide smile on my face. Thank you for believing in me. I sure do love you.

Barb Osburn: The Lord knew I needed you, and I am indebted to you. Your gentle and tender shepherding of my heart has always lifted me up toward Jesus, and I wouldn't be where or who I am without you. Forever gratefulness is my song.

Kathryn Shindoll and Marissa Meinema: Thank you for being rocks in my life. I have unwavering confidence in your friendship, and I could not think of better women to walk through this life with, even from across the world. Kathryn, you are the best godmother to my Carmel, and I'm so thankful you shared her homecoming with me. Riss, you are a worshiper, and so much of who you are in the Lord I hope for Miah to be someday. Your voice and your heart to lead worship have given great vision to Miah, and she adores you. You both amaze me.

Jordyn Osburn: Your commitment to me and to the writing of this book has blessed me deeply. Thank you for your comments, critiques, and suggestions concerning this manuscript. Yours were the first set of eyes to read part of this work, and I'll always rejoice in that. Thank you for the way you love Jesus.

Brian Stone, Amie Whittington, and Kayla Kasica: Thank you for being three of the four (Barb Osburn was the other) who stood with me in the toughest moments of my obedience. Your certainty in what the Lord was asking me to do was a gift I desperately needed. When everyone else said no, your yes made all the difference. Thank you for adding your faith to mine. You are heroes.

Kevin and Tina DeKam: You two are a drink of cool water and a safe place for me and my girls to land. I will always stand in absolute awe of how Jesus knit our stories together, especially through Teya's adoption, and I am forever humbled by how gracious you have been to me. I love and trust you both.

My big Zambian family: You have changed my life forever. Thank you for being not just eager but ecstatic about this book, and thank you for letting me tell these stories. I cannot wait to see Jesus garment you with glory and reveal to you all the riches you've stored up in heaven. I'm so grateful we'll get to be together forever in the age to come. I look forward to amazing chocolates and the biggest pillow fights forever! You are beautiful to me.

My intercessor team: Thank you for standing in the gap for me. Thank you for not picking up fear over my life when the unimaginable has happened, and thank you for the quality of your devotion to me. Your bold intercession has carried me.

My love, my carpenter, my groom forever: Jesus, You are the one all this is for. Your faithfulness leaves me in the deepest awe. I weep at the sound of Your voice. You surely know me better than I know myself and knew I desperately needed Your rescue. Thank You for giving me the memory of my first secret place with You where You marked me as Your own, and thank You for showing me Yourself so fully. Oh, that these words would somehow reverberate in the nations—testifying wholly of You, the only one worthy to open the scroll.

The Zambian soil is so familiar—the smell as it brushes by my nose leaves me lingering, eager for more.

I cannot help but take off my shoes to feel that ground—hard and dry, yet so full of life, energizing me through the bare soles of my feet.

Part 1

SLOW OBEDIENCE IS NO OBEDIENCE

"If you love me, keep my commands."

—John 14:15

"Whoever has my commands and keeps them is the one who loves me."

—John 14:21

CHAPTER

YES

June 2009

"You want me here?" I asked Him, startled.

My nineteen-year-old body lay violently shivering in my bed due to the cold Zambian night. I had been adjusting to life in a small compound called Kalingalinga, enjoying the opportunity to work with orphaned children every day. Earlier in the year I had been selected for an internship with a ministry in the nation of Zambia, and my main responsibilities involved orphan sponsorship. The first two months of my internship had flown by, and the programs to which I had been assigned were going exceptionally well. I had been able to get multiple child sponsorship updates done each day, and a stack of the children's letters and testimonies for their sponsors were collecting dust at my bedside. Although I was in a foreign nation, away from all the first-world comforts to which I was so accustomed, my life had a surprising degree of order and predictability.

"You want me here? I already am here. What do you mean?" I questioned Him again. I turned to see if someone was in the room, only to find the glossy cream walls staring back at me. I shut my Bible, as if

3

to make a point that I was done with Jesus for the evening, only again to hear His voice so clearly it was almost audible. Slightly annoyed, I lifted the covers and pulled them tightly over my right shoulder. My head collapsed back into the pillow except it no longer felt like a pillow. It was cold and stiff, harsh on hope for a good night's sleep.

I lay there for what seemed like hours, feeling confused and uncertain. If it was Jesus speaking rather than just a thought in my head, what could He possibly mean by saying that He wanted me here? I already was here. I was already invested in Zambia, taking part in the work He had set before me. *It must be the side effects of my malaria pills*, I thought, trying to pacify my concern. Again I rolled over, trying to reposition my head and my body to find comfort. Nothing.

Screams from women outside accompanied the breeze, which leaked through the barred windows into my room. My fear intensified as I listened. What was going on outside? What was happening, even in here? "Jesus!" I finally cried out. "Lord, if it's You, I'm up! I'm up!" I slid my hand down the side of my bed into the side pocket of my backpack. I groped around, my fingers trying to find the flashlight that I had put away hours earlier. "Aha!" I whispered as I finally got a hold of it. I grabbed my Bible too, figuring I'd need that as well. The night now seemed young, though moments before the time had aged past 3:00 a.m.

The Holy Spirit prompted me to turn to the book of Esther, and somehow I understood that it would reveal an invitation that Jesus was extending to me. I knew I could not ignore Him, so I opened to Esther. I began reading, knowing that whatever it was that He wanted me to understand, He would make it stand out, almost as if the font were in bold, uppercase letters. After reading the first three chapters somewhat carelessly, I arrived at chapter 4, which says, "For if you remain silent at this time, relief and deliverance for the Jews will arise from another place, but you and your father's family will perish. And who knows but that you have come to your royal position for such a time as this?" (Esther 4:14).

It was as if I would never need the instruction again. I understood from that small portion of Scripture, without one more spoken word from Jesus, that this was His way of demonstrating that He had prepared a place and an opportunity for me here in Zambia and that I now had a choice. I could choose obedience or disobedience.

I could choose to remain silent, writing off His intimate invitation and letting Him call someone else to accomplish what He was asking. Or I could choose to believe that He had called me specifically and had prepared a way for such a time as this. I knew without a doubt that not only would this call affect my life and the lives of many in Zambia, but that my decision to obey Jesus and to follow Him as He led me to Zambia would quite possibly have an even more dramatic effect and leave a heavenly mark on my family. I understood that I needed to soberly count the cost, since this decision would reap huge consequences for my family and my community.

Images of leaving my upper-class education and culture and stepping into the dusty lives of children deemed filth triggered thoughts of a Scripture passage I had read time and time again: "Speak up for those who cannot speak for themselves, for the rights of all who are destitute. Speak up and judge fairly; defend the rights of the poor and needy" (Proverbs 31:8–9).

Was this the voice Jesus was calling me to use?

Though I knew in my spirit that this was indeed what Jesus was calling me to do, the prospect was agonizing for my flesh. I trembled at the thought of leaving college two and a half years prematurely. *What about my friends? What about my family?* I wondered. *How is this going to work?* I ached at the idea of leaving my friends, and my insides burned as I thought about giving up the comforts of home and my relationships. I begged Jesus to give me courage to deliberately say yes, but doing this hurt deeply. At the core of my being, I already knew my yes was His; I couldn't resist Him, but my flesh despised the thought. My skin felt like it was splitting, being stretched and torn with searing pain, and I hated the war within me. My spirit's simple yes seemed effortlessly at peace, while my flesh trembled, fighting in opposition. *Jesus, my family? Will they ever understand? How can I do this? How can I deny them? How can I turn from my father's house and run?* I wept uncontrollably.

5

My exhaustive questioning finally came to a halt, and in my flesh's surrender I humbly mirrored Mary's response recorded in the book of Luke. I cried out to Him, "I am your servant. May your word to me be fulfilled" (Luke 1:38).

The sun shone in my room, revealing its warmth. Comfort surrounded me as I embraced peace and the fruit of sweet surrender. With my face directly on the concrete floor and tears flooding beneath, I understood that as a nineteen-year-old single woman, I would become a full-time missionary in Zambia.

Missionaries are just ordinary people who say yes to Jesus.

CHAPTER

2

THE HARDEST CONVERSATION

I saw my dad first since his head stood much taller than anyone else's in the crowd of people waiting outside of customs. Anxious excitement came over me as I approached my family, though I also felt fear deep inside. Bear hugs were in store, especially for my little sister. My mom's embrace was sweet, and one of my longtime friends had me laughing within seconds. It felt so good to be back in America, but already my heart was no longer wholly willing to call America home. The strong ache in my stomach that felt like homesickness was for another country—a land where children ran freely and dust filled every crevice, a place so different and foreign, yet one where heaven met earth more clearly than I had ever seen before.

I assumed no one around me would understand. I was pretty sure that no matter how gently I explained it, there would still be more questions than answers. I felt in my heart that if I waited to tell my family members, I could not answer their questions honestly. I couldn't tell them how my internship had been without telling them what Jesus was so intimately calling me to do. I longed for them to understand and to see Jesus's hand at work in my life. I craved my family's support, but I didn't have the slightest idea how to approach this conversation.

That long Zambian night kept returning to the forefront of my mind, reminding me that I had been given an invitation, not a mandate. It was a gift to choose obedience.

I didn't know how to be vulnerable, and to a more-than-usual degree I could sense the walls going up around my heart. I wasn't afraid of saying yes to Zambia, but I was terrified that my yes would hurt others. I began to feel calloused and cold—even trapped. I felt isolated from everyone, petrified at the possibility of confusion and disapproval. And I wondered if my obedience would stand the test of the conversation before me.

With smiles and happy hearts, we piled into the car. My dad lifted my luggage into the spacious trunk, and I couldn't help but widen my cheeks in an enormous smile. What none of them knew was that those bags were full of Zambian gifts that I had brought for them and for so many other people I loved. I imagined that later that evening I'd see my mother smile as I pulled out lovely Zambian fabrics I couldn't wait to show her and the tenderly carved and colorful jewelry that I had picked out for many of my friends. I also had letters that I had kept throughout my time in Zambia for each member of my family. Every letter was much more than prose on a page; it was love extended, a longing to invite my family into my heart and to journey with Jesus in Zambia.

I snuggled in between my friend and my sister, still wearing my *chitenge*, a piece of Zambian material often worn as a skirt. I was jittery and excited, scared and overwhelmed at the thought that we would be together in the car for the next three hours. In Zambia I had anticipated the day when I could again have smoothies and ice cream, pizza and french fries, but adrenaline and nerves had completely squelched my cravings.

I felt culture shock as I saw the strategically designed roads and exit ramps. My mind flashed back to dusty roads filled with foot-deep potholes. I stared at BMWs, Lexus SUVs, and Hummers, all with busy drivers, multi-tasking and carrying on with their normal lives, and I couldn't help but think about hundreds of Zambians lining the sides of streets, walking everywhere. Billboards flashed with messages promising "Your best life now!" and I wondered about the millions of people in Zambia who would celebrate their "best life now" with a day's worth of wages to provide enough food for their families. Other billboards said, "Only $1" and "For once, just think about yourself," and my stomach turned. I couldn't help but think how a single dollar would have to feed entire families the same night.

My mind had spun in circles the entire forty-hour journey back to the States and even more so now that I was with my family. My insides churned violently as I wondered, *Should I let time pass? Ease my way back into life with everyone and then tell them? Or should I just tell them now so they have ample time for the news to sink in?* I didn't know how to handle all that I was feeling inside, and I felt like I was doing a terrible job of hiding the turmoil within me. I was certain that I would return to Zambia, but somehow, making a choice that would cause others pain left me feeling like the biggest coward. I was terribly unsettled. I couldn't figure out how to have this conversation, and I felt the weight of the world on my shoulders.

I grew nauseous with concern for my parents and the grief they didn't know was coming. I knew the news would be hard no matter what way I told them, and I was sure this conversation would mark the beginning of a deep and potentially lasting ache in their hearts. I was beside myself with fear, and I couldn't hold it in.

"I'm going back," I said. "Jesus wants me to leave college and lay down everything. I'm moving to Zambia."

I shut my eyes and put my arm around my little sister's shoulder. My hometown in southwest Michigan seemed farther away from Chicago than it had ever been before.

∽

I was full of anticipation, anxiously straining to spot my big sister come through the doors of customs. It had been months since we had seen her. On my tiptoes, I saw Sophie walking through a towering doorway, given away by her bright blond hair and her beaming smile. She rolled two large suitcases behind her, and she was wrapped in colorful Zambian fabric. Our large posters plastered with the message "Welcome home, Sophie!" crashed to the floor, and the international terminal seemed to stand still for a moment. We ran to greet her, so thankful to have our Sophie back for the first time in months, safe and sound in America. It seemed nothing had changed.

A three-hour drive home awaited us as we packed into the Honda Pilot. While her friend sat at her left side, I clung to Sophie's right side the entire ride, wide-eyed and in awe of my big sister, who looked like an African princess. Mom and Dad couldn't help but look in the rearview mirror one too many times, comforted by that beautiful smile they hadn't seen in so long. "How was it?" "Did you make friends from the program?" "How were the children?" they asked. Sophie did everything she could to explain her previous months, yet I could sense by her hesitancy that there was something going on inside of her. Though the excitement was undeniable, I was nervous. It seemed like I was the only one who could feel this tension.

Eventually our conversation stilled as raindrops gently fell on the windshield. I could tell that Sophie was tired and that her heart was heavy with what must have felt impossible to articulate. "I think ..." She paused. "I'm going back," she finally blurted out. My heart shattered. I looked to my sister, hoping in vain to grab on to any ounce of certainty that I could. I felt an immediate emptiness in my spirit, and I began to shut down completely. Truth became relative and fickle.

Waves of fighting and tears were followed by silence and sorrow. Three hours seemed like an eternity; the car ride was a blur, and that was only the beginning. It was as if thunderclouds had rolled in to stay and I was lost under a dark haze. Though it wouldn't last forever, I couldn't bring myself to approach a God whose name brought such division to our family. Confusion paralyzed me.

As we moved forward no one knew what the future would hold. As Sophie's sister, I felt an intense paradox: sometimes I was proud of her, but mostly I was hurt and terrified. I knew no more than Sophie what was to come, and yet, unbeknownst to me, the Lord had perfectly worked out the timing. Jesus had an extraordinary plan for Sophie, and her life of obedience would disrupt, change, and mark my life and our family forever.

CHAPTER

Let Love Cover

As the news that I was moving to Zambia became more public, the ache within me became increasingly unbearable. The testing of my faith had never been so intimidating and so drenched in the spirit of fear. Though choosing obedience wasn't necessarily scary for me, fear had gripped the hearts of many who loved me, making it only natural to respond in what must have felt like a traumatic way to them. It was hard for me to maintain confidence and humility, because lies were swarming in my mind too. I would fall asleep at night hearing in second person, *Sophie, you're so stubborn. You make such impulsive decisions, and a decision made in the name of Jesus is no different. You're such a deceiver. All you do is cause people pain. You have been and always will be a burden.*

I would stay up deep into the night, often fearful of what the next day would bring. As I cried out to Jesus night after night, I knew with complete certainty that this decision was of Him, but I hated not feeling understood. I wanted desperately for Him to lift the burden from my family and my community and to tell them that my return to Zambia indeed would be used for everyone's good. I wanted His promises to come alive in their lives and for peace that passes understanding to come over them, washing away all the fear. As the weeks passed, though, the

11

situation kept worsening. My decision was challenging the rapport my family had with the community, and I was purposefully becoming more withdrawn.

One evening sweat dripped down my back as I gripped the carpet in my bedroom. My mouth tasted sour, almost foaming as my body heaved. Unable to hold up my head, I surrendered completely to the floor. Belly down and face in the carpet, I wept—hard.

"Jesus, if You don't tell me again today that You want me in Zambia, I don't know if I can do it! How long can I bear this affliction? How long, O Lord? Jesus, remind me again who You are and what You are inviting me to do! Help my family! Wrap Your arms around us!" Though I longed to see Jesus lead me forth into His will for me in Zambia, these were my deep cries. This was the hardest season I knew, one of pinpointing and harassment, deep questioning and intrusive accusation.

The time was nearing for me to return to college where I would spend my last few months before going back to Zambia. Though I tried mightily to pretend that obedience was clean and easy, life was hard. Insults and questions were frequently hurled my way, and my family couldn't escape the interrogations either. One day just a week or so before my return to college, a believer very near to me aggressively questioned my decision.

"What do you know about helping people in Africa? And how do you think you can handle all of the poverty and the horrible situations when you have never experienced that? You will not be safe, and all I'll be able to say when you come home is, 'I told you so.'"

Conversations like this left me almost speechless, hurting and feeling like I had no voice. I felt threatened and pressured to have the perfect explanation. I spent a great deal of energy constantly trying to explain myself, but nothing helped. Nothing I said could tame the fear in those who loved me. And though I wanted them to feel otherwise, I couldn't blame them. They were hurting too.

My anxiety was debilitating, and I ached for my family members to be free of the weight of my decision—and to be free of me. All I could think about was how much of a burden I was to them and how I wished there was something I could do to alleviate all the pain I was causing them. The pressure was too heavy. No one could possibly understand how I felt.

I continued to grieve, and week after week I felt emotionally slaughtered because of my decision to obey. Despite my daily need for Him to reaffirm His will, I knew what Jesus was calling me to do. Still, I didn't want to be the only one who believed this was the narrow road He was calling me to take. Isolation is not a safe place to be.

By the time the summer was over, four people had joined me in believing that Jesus was setting the nation of Zambia before me—one pastor, one mentor, one friend, and one woman whom I adored as a big-sister figure. I was thankful for them and I cherished them. I clung to them and the encouraging words they spoke. I read and reread their emails and listened to the messages they left on my phone and in my Bible. I thanked Jesus for the grace of their presence and for the counsel of their lips. Their love kept me strong, and their allegiance to Jesus kept me pressing onward.

I made it back to college and found my friends and my sweet mentor there. The campus was fresh, worship was alive, and I was in a community of people who better than anyone knew the depth of my love for Jesus. I hoped that my last few months in the States would be a season away with the Lord, though all I wanted was to be back in Zambia. Before classes started, I got in a groove by running with one of my best friends, and that was an excellent escape from the heaviness I was carrying. My faith seemed to soar in this community, and I believed this would be a season marked with Jesus's faithfulness, His abundant provision, and restoration straight from His hand. I also believed the Lord would open specific doors for me in Zambia and commission me more definitively for the work He had set before me.

Despite all the hope and excitement, longing marked my days— extreme longing for a country, for a people, and for a specific land to know the name of Jesus. I wrote in my journal,

> I just want to be there. I'm so homesick for the air, the dust,
> and the children. I am so lost, part of me here yet all of me still

there. Oh Jesus, Zambia—I am so unworthy to hold this heart. How, honestly, can I stay here any longer? How can I stand to wait one more day? How can I even hope? "Oh that I might have my request, and that God would grant me the thing I long for. What strength I have left, that I should wait and hope? And what is ahead of me, that I should be patient?" (Job 8:11)

Fundraising was also a part of my last few months in the States. I had no strategy, other than to share my heart and to trust that the Lord would prompt people to give. I talked to a few friends about arranging small fundraisers, but no major opportunities had presented themselves. Though I knew I needed money, I was so convinced that Jesus wanted me in Zambia that I was prepared to go even if I didn't have any. One night in August, I had a dream that I was sitting on top of my bags at the airport, penniless and simply waiting. Jesus had said that someone would buy me a plane ticket to Zambia, and so I waited there, packed and ready. This dream reflected my ever-increasing faith that regardless of the outcome of my fundraising attempts, I would make it to Zambia with provision straight from the Lord's hand. If the time came for me to leave and I had no money, I would pack my bags and go to the airport. I would wait at the ticketing gate, no matter how long it took, and Jesus would send someone to pay for my ticket. I believed in His faithfulness.

One night in late September, something amazing happened. It had been a terribly difficult week, and I had so much on my mind as the time wound down. I heard about a worship night taking place downtown, and I decided to go. I invited a friend and we left shortly after. The evening began with worship led by a small band made up of older men. I knew the moment I stepped inside the room that Jesus was going to touch my heart and lavish me with His fierce love.

Worship brought me to tears and to my knees. The name of Jesus on my tongue was so sweet, and my vocal chords acted as if they had been pumped with steroids. The voices of all those in the room must have echoed down the streets, and the instruments were thunderous. The service was beautiful. The night was sweet and still so young.

As worship continued, a twenty-two-year-old man got up to share a word. He said that at age seventeen, Jesus had called him to the Democratic Republic of the Congo and that he went, saying yes to Jesus all the way. In testimony after testimony he told about the Lord's gracious provision, care, everlasting mercy, and unfailing love, which he had seen firsthand in Congo. It was obvious that this man, though young, was completely led by the Holy Spirit and in submission to Him. I was encouraged and excited, thankful to be in an atmosphere of such faith.

Silence filled the room as he wrapped up the word he had prepared to share. In a sweetly intimate moment with Jesus, I felt Him lead me to walk toward the front. Within seconds, I was standing directly before this young man and I had lost sight of everyone else in the room. With no hesitancy I shared with him everything that the Lord was calling me to do. I was unable to talk fast enough.

"He has called me to Zambia. I was there and then He told me He wants me to move there. I'm still in college, but I'm leaving—soon. He's called me to be a mother in this nation. He's called me to serve these children and to be a voice for those who have no voice. It's crazy. Most of my friends and family are trying to stop me from going, but I can't say no. I love Jesus. I love Him. I love Him. Oh I love Him!" I fell to the floor in tears, and the man began to pray. His prayers were precise, filled with deep wells of wisdom that came from experiencing the character of God. He spoke portions of Scripture over me but suddenly stopped when he also fell to the floor and began weeping.

"Oh Lord, this heart. Oh Jesus, she is yours. Her heart belongs to you. Yes, Lord. Yes. Oh Jesus! Yes!" This must have gone on for some time, because I heard more voices reverberating in the room, joining in prayer for me. I was humbled to the core and thankful since I had never been the recipient of such a corporate covering.

After some time, I slowly raised my head. My back was heavy, with hands laid all across it, and my face was dripping a mixture of salty tears and thick mucus. A large group of people had surrounded me, all of them petitioning the Lord on my behalf. Some were laughing. Some were weeping. Some were shouting bold declarations. Some were singing. And some even seemed to have picked up the burden of agony I was carrying—they were groaning.

I was so overwhelmed by the love being poured out over me that I placed my head back down. Moments later, a man and a woman brought me to my feet and said they wanted to pray for me because they felt that Jesus wanted them to tell me something. The man reached for his wallet, grabbed a dollar bill, and ripped it into many pieces. He then placed all the pieces in my hand and said, "Money doesn't matter. Jesus matters." Then his wife began praying, and through laughter she said, "Jesus has already told you where He wants to send you. It is a country. Yes, He's given you a place. What is it?"

"Zambia," I said. They exploded in laughter and the woman began crying. She reached out her hand and grabbed mine, saying, "We were missionaries in Zambia for seven years! Oh Jesus, wow!" The three of us talked and prayed for a while, discussing particulars about Zambia, and I clung to every word that came from their mouths. They were wise. They had been there. They knew the ground. They knew the dust. They knew the children who had so captured my heart.

As our conversation ended, I quietly retreated to sing a song of gratitude to Jesus. I reveled in His presence and couldn't believe what He alone had orchestrated in a single evening. Though I am sure that each person found freedom in God's presence that night, everything seemed intimately planned for me. My heart was moved and my faith was strengthened by leaning into the embrace of a God who knows me.

As my friend and I left, we were given a free pizza at the door. We ran through the streets, praising Jesus openly. We were completely caught up in the joy of His name. We were thankful. We couldn't believe what had happened while also believing it completely. "Jesus, thank you! You are just too good," I said with laughter.

I arrived home with a full heart. I was blessed and encouraged, knowing that though my life was about to change drastically, Jesus would be faithful to me. He not only had spoken directly to me and confirmed that I was to be in Zambia, but He had put me in the same room with two seasoned missionaries from that country who shared their wisdom and prayed over me. I was also completely humbled by the testimonies the speaker had shared, knowing he was sent specifically by Jesus to sow seeds of expectation in my heart for what was to come.

That expectation led me to the floor where my face again met the carpet. This time, though, I wasn't mourning. Instead, I was rejoicing in the faithfulness of Jesus and in the promise that I would see His glory in the days to come.

And I knew that in grievance and in glory, His love would cover all.

CHAPTER 4

FLIGHT 254

The day my sister left for Zambia I felt melancholy, and her departure affected every facet of my life. School was a blur behind my constant tears, and I played the worst basketball game of my life. I was completely absent and distracted from everything; I was just going through the motions. Anything said to me entered one ear and immediately exited the other. All I wanted was to have more time with my sister. I wished someone understood the hurt that my family carried, the judgment we encountered daily, and the interrogations we faced. I didn't know what or whom to believe. As much as I craved to be understood, I had no clarity myself. Somewhere deep within me I wanted to believe that this was the Lord's will and therefore to stand by my sister against popular opinion. However, I felt hurt and harbored resentment toward Jesus and my sister. I was weak and aimless.

A constant inner dialogue exhausted me. I wearied at each question and comment. *Why doesn't she finish school first? She only has two and a half years left. This always happens when people go on mission trips—eventually they come down from their high. What do you mean that's where she's being called? How do you feel about her leaving you, Sam? She's going to miss the end of your high school career. That's not fair to you.*

I defended my sister in public, but I was asking myself the same questions others were. I was in a never-ending tug-of-war in which I was the object being tugged. Sophie was firm and confident, and she gently tried to help me understand her perspective by walking through all the questions that I had or that people had asked me. I desperately tried to cling to her surety that this was indeed God's will for her. Sometimes in an effort to protect Sophie, I hid the fact that I was bombarded with these interrogations each day. I was subject to the emotion of the day.

These comments occupied my sixteen-year-old mind for months. Everything Sophie was doing contradicted my sense of normalcy. I struggled with the Lord, asking, "Why me? Why my sister? Why now? My family is in shambles, and my mind is being constantly yanked around. God, why?"

The only thing that seemed to nurture my relationship with the Lord in these difficult months was the little communication my sister and I had once she arrived in Zambia. When I heard her voice or read her messages, I grew in confidence that this was what Jesus had set before her. Her calling began to make more sense to me, and I started to tune out people and to be proud of my big sister. This was a long time coming, but the more I opened my heart to Jesus, the more I understood. I knew Sophie loved Him, because she took His commands seriously (John 14:15). But I just had never thought that following Jesus could cause so much pain.

The day came to leave. So much had happened in the last few months, and a plethora of emotions and buckets of adrenaline fueled my every moment. I was excited and energized, but I also was devastated and exhausted. I had said good-bye to my family two days before, with wounds freshly stinging and searing me deeply. My parents had not given their blessing for me to go, and their denial and disbelief must have had them repeating, "This is not really happening" over and over in their heads. Sleepless nights plagued me as I desperately cried out for my family, hoping they might understand that it truly was Jesus calling me to Zambia. Though I prayed earnestly that He would cover them in those moments of fear and doubt, I knew that one day they would see

Him as the author of my story and would bless His name for what He had done in sending me to Zambia.

As I said good-bye to my little college home, my dear friends helped me load the car. It was a moment worth remembering, almost surreal as we pulled out of my driveway one last time. I squeezed my housemates with a promise to see them again, though I didn't know when that would be, if ever. Tears revealing the intensity of my emotions fell from my eyes, and all I could do was pray. I anticipated the final good-byes I would have to say to two of my dearest friends at the airport and knew that the forty-hour journey back to Zambia could be full of anguish. *Jesus, is this really what You have called me to do?* I wondered.

I felt like I was going a little bit crazy. I wondered, *How can I be so certain that this is what Jesus has for me and be so excited about it while at the same time being so sad and so desperate for my life to be normal?* I had been longing to return to Zambia, but now that the day of my departure had come, I couldn't believe I would be there so soon. I wanted more time. My life seemed so atypical. Those voices saying, *Why can't you go after college? After you graduate?* planted themselves in my mind, their roots digging deeper. As we drove, I realized how hard it was going to be to actually get on that plane.

I will never forget those three hours on the road. I watched the signs. I watched the cars. I stared at my friends. We talked, cried, and laughed. Our conversation resembled our normal heart-to-heart talks about Jesus. It was almost like any other day, but it definitely wasn't. Everything I knew was nearing an abrupt end.

Relationships were all I could think about, specifically those I was leaving behind. Over and over I counted the cost, and never in my life had my yes to Jesus felt so weak, so frail. I debated whether I could lay down everything, including the people I loved the most, for the sake of making Jesus's name known. It was my joy to lay down everything for Jesus's sake, but I struggled to wholly embrace doing this without picking up offense. I understood far more than I ever had what Jesus meant when He commanded His followers to pick up their crosses and to follow Him. This was difficult. Though I had been living in passionate pursuit of Jesus for a few years, I felt I was picking up my cross for the first time. And I was awfully weak.

For a little while, I felt as if something was being stolen from me. The moments in the car with my precious friends were fleeting, and I felt as if someone was yanking them away. They were almost eerie, filled with pain that weighed heavily on us all, and yet there was a catch, one I could not shake: I was the one who had chosen love. I had chosen obedience. No one was stealing these moments from me and no one was making me go. My beloved Jesus had simply gifted me with an invitation to go, and by His grace, I was willing to follow. In His kindness, I wanted His will. Up to this point, His mercy and faithfulness had accompanied my every move, and I knew that despite my tiny and frail yes, His presence would remain forever. He would keep me and He would bless me.

"Welcome to Chicago O'Hare," the sign read. It felt like a knife had wedged itself in the pit of my stomach.

We unloaded the car. My orange suitcases, packed precisely and easily recognizable, came first. I thought about all that I had packed inside, how these were my only possessions but they meant so little to me. I briefly imagined unpacking everything and leaving all of my things strewn throughout the airport parking lot to make room for my dear friends to be packed inside. I wondered what would happen if I missed my flight or if security detained me. I secretly hoped for something to happen, maybe a flight delay or even cancelation, but then I remembered. *Dusty streets. Precious children. Oh, the smell of that Zambian air.*

"Good-bye," I said numbly as I held on to my sweet friend. "I love you," I whispered, tears streaming down my cheeks. "I can't believe I am going." Moments passed and I pulled back from our embrace, saying, "I'll see you soon." Though I knew I wouldn't see her soon, it didn't matter. Now was not the time to face that pain.

I turned to my other dear friend and nearly collapsed into her arms. My body convulsed and I wept hard. She began crying too. I held on to her tightly, pleading with God in my mind. I begged Him to whisper, "Well done, Sophie. I just wanted to see that you were willing. You can go back home now." But no such fantasy transpired. I could see the gate, and it was time to go.

"I love you," I cried as I buried my head in her shoulder one more time.

"I love you too, Sophie. I'll see you soon," she said. I walked back to my other friend and gave her one more hug. I held on tightly, and without words, we parted. As I walked away, they watched until I was out of sight.

∞

I boarded the plane, tears still streaming. Quietly I found my seat, placed my handbag on the floor, and sat down. I looked around. Vacationers and businesspeople surrounded me, all of whom, I assumed, would reach their final destinations in Europe. Young girls about my age, decorated in fun jewelry and wearing scarves and "I heart Chicago" T-shirts, walked by, talking and laughing and reminiscing about their soon-to-end American vacation. In contrast, my face was blotchy and red, and because I didn't want anyone to notice me (and the very obvious part of me that was mourning), I turned toward the window and reclined my seat. At least I could hide my face and pretend to sleep until the stewardess came around and asked me to put my seat up.

I turned on my iPod, needing desperately to quiet my soul and to lose myself in worship. I chose a playlist of my favorite worship artist, who carries an anointing that always ushers me into authenticity before Jesus, and that was what I needed. I had fifty-eight of her songs and I planned to listen to all of them over and over until I made it first to London and then to Zambia. Moments later, the stewardess tapped my shoulder as expected. I put my seat up and turned off my iPod, and soon we were on the runway. I took out a piece of spearmint gum and forced it into my mouth. Plagued with nausea and exhaustion, I pulled out a pen and wrote on the gum wrapper, "This is all because I love you, Jesus."

I was desperate. I was broken and mourning. I was contrite in spirit and heavy laden, but I longed to love the One who was worthy. I longed to share with Jesus the brokenness of my heart and still praise Him in it. And then it came, a song I hadn't heard before. For the rest of the flight, all ten hours and thirty-six minutes, I listened to one song on repeat that captured it all. Wasting my life on Jesus. He was the one I was after.

∞

The flight landed on time, leaving a daunting twelve-hour layover in London's Heathrow Airport ahead of me. I was in and out of sleep for the majority of the flight, and I was somber. Despite the constant stream of people lugging their bags through the terminals, I was able to focus and to delight in the presence of Jesus. I was not distracted but instead was caught up in a peace so real it was almost tangible. In my journal I wrote,

> Jesus, here I am. I am in London Heathrow. Wow. I just come; I'm calm and focused on You. Open Your floodgates. Let Your love pour out on me. Spirit, come; reside here in me, Your temple. I proclaim my identity as Your bride. All I want is for You to have Your way.
>
> Holy Spirit, I want Your tangible presence. I long for You. My stomach leaps, thinking about Your touch. My heart bubbles with joy, knowing how You love me. Wow. How beautiful.
>
> Weeping endured through the night, but joy comes in the morning. Deep cries out to deep. Oh Lord, grant me a spirit of peace, not of worry, trusting that Your voice and Your face are not hidden from me.

The time passed slowly as I waited for my next flight. The airport seesawed back and forth from a chaotic craze to a dull hum of people moving about. It had quieted again as evening approached, and I was eager to board my last flight before touching down in Zambia's capital, the city of Lusaka.

Boarding was surreal, knowing the next time I touched the ground it would be on Zambian soil. I couldn't wait to smell the dusty air and to see the deep blue African sky again. As the plane took off and settled at the ideal altitude, I put on my headphones and immediately fell asleep.

I woke after an hour or so, only to sit and wait for the next nine hours. I was tired but too jittery to sleep anymore. The good-byes I had said the day before seemed forever in the past, and despite the wounds I still felt, I had turned the page. In an evening's time, I would be back on Zambian soil.

The sun began to shine above the clouds about an hour out from my final destination. Reaching down beside my swollen ankles, I felt around to find my journal and a pen. One more entry was necessary before arriving in Zambia. I knew this was a moment worth remembering.

> Just moments away from landing. I'm exhausted. Yet I am too eager to rest anymore. I look out and see the bright sun raised above the clouds. Jesus, I feel close. I can taste the warmth of Your presence, Your joy continuing to fill my being. My mind races, wondering how I am actually here, how in just a few minutes I will touch down in Zambia again. How beautiful and how precious this return.
>
> My mouth is filled with praises for something other than this return, though. Jesus, I love You. I love You all the way. I am so touched by Your love, so touched by Your Spirit, so richly blessed by Your presence. Oh Jesus, how I love You.
>
> Jesus, Your love has no bounds. Jesus, Your love is more faithful than the morning. Next time I write, I will actually be in Zambia! Wow!

Moments later, I set foot in Zambia. Jesus had been faithful to bring me back to the place I loved, and my heart leapt in gratitude. All that I had been through, both struggle and triumph, peaked in this moment. His faithfulness had carried me, and all I could see was how beautiful He was.

PART 2

HUNGRY AND BROKEN

"Blessed are the poor in spirit, for theirs is the kingdom of heaven. Blessed are those who mourn, for they will be comforted. Blessed are the meek, for they will inherit the earth. Blessed are those who hunger and thirst for righteousness, for they will be filled."

—Matthew 5:3–6

CHAPTER

MY BROKENNESS BEFORE ME

I really am here, Jesus. I am abruptly being confronted with this reality. I am desperate for You, longing for You. I'm here in Zambia. This is my life now. But Jesus, I need You to be my life. If that's true, then my life hasn't changed. Jesus, I want You more. I need You. I need Your touch and Your voice—Your Word to strengthen me. I need Your Spirit to be noticeably present. I need You to be my comfort, my longing, my peace, my joy. I need a spirit of prayer to loom over me always. I need to know that You are always with me.

My arrival in Zambia brought to the surface an avalanche of emotions. Fear and the daunting thought that this was my life now contrasted starkly with what I had imagined my return would be. The African heat enveloped me completely, and the conditions of my new home intimidated me. The cement blocks with the blotchy, charred-black paint looked different from my clean suburban siding. The bars over my windows and the twelve-foot cement wall (topped with broken glass bottles) that enclosed the entire plot were a far cry from my open yard with green grass. The black metal gate with several padlocks screamed of a need for heightened security, unlike my screen door, which didn't even have a lock. The dusty streets didn't feel foreign, but they weren't hosting any welcome-home celebrations either.

After a few days had passed and I was beginning to acclimate a bit, I sat down at my computer to check my email for the first time. I had a picture and a list of things that Jesus was already doing that I was eager to share, and I was excited to connect with people back home. I hoped to find one of my friends or my little sister on chat so we could touch base and talk a bit.

I plugged the long blue cord into the side of my computer and patiently waited for the Internet to connect. My Bible sat beside me as did my camera, and I scrolled through the few pictures that I had already uploaded onto my computer. After a few minutes, I smiled as I noticed that the Internet had connected, and I immediately logged into my email, eager to find messages from loved ones. Instead of joyous encouragement from friends, the first email I opened informed me of an awful tragedy that had taken the lives of two students from my college.

One of them was a classmate and a friend of mine. Gone.

I wept through the night. I wept hard. I felt helpless, so far from being able to do anything. I felt lost. I was devastated and without consolation. I couldn't free myself from the grip that absolute grief and fear had on me. I kept crying out and I wrote sloppily in my journal, "Jesus, is this real? I'm sad. I'm lost. I'm scared. She was twenty. I don't understand. I am so deeply saddened. I wish I could be there. I offer myself as a sacrifice, though, in all of this. Lord, may my suffering honor You. May my lonely cries be heard, and somehow, may my mourning glorify You. I'm weak and I'm poor. I'm oh so sad, but I am Yours."

※

I could not have prepared myself for the grief of that day or for the waves of grief that would follow in the months to come. Since I had said my good-byes only days before, I still felt closely connected, but now I was far removed. I couldn't grasp the reality of such a loss while being so distant and isolated from my community. The physical realities of living in sub-Saharan Africa (like often having no electricity or water) yielded no comfort, and I fell into a deep, depressive grief. I often thought, *If this is my introduction to learning how to depend on you Lord, wow.* His wounding felt harsh, and I was being stripped of everything.

In the few moments of rest I had each day that I didn't spend curled up crying in my room or wishing I could be back in college with my friends, I meditated on the Beatitudes and on the opening chapters of the Sermon on the Mount (Matthew 5, 6). I wasn't interested in the cliché verses about suffering, so I began praying that the Lord would open my eyes in a new way, that I would see His Word and power afresh. I wanted to dive into Scripture with new hunger and new yearning, believing that somehow He would restore life to my sad and weary soul.

With each day that passed, simple things began to give me tangible support. The three-room house that I shared with another missionary felt more like home, and the ministry happening there (the home doubled as a service center) was encouraging. Women and children filed in and out each day, craving anything that we were able and willing to give. Some days we would teach English; other days they would teach us Nyanja. Some days we would stop everything and pray and study Scripture. Some days we went into the compounds, evangelizing and visiting homes, and other days we would sing and dance. Some days we would cook and clean. It was obvious that all of us were becoming family.

One Friday the Lord woke me up with the Word in Isaiah 58. He spoke clearly to me, asking me to gather the women to fast and saying that in obedience we would see His glory. We had been fasting on Fridays, but on this day, Jesus had made it clear to me that He had something specific in mind for us. When all the women gathered I shared this:

> Is not this the kind of fasting I have chosen: to loose the chains of injustice and untie the cords of the yoke, to set the oppressed free and break every yoke? Is it not to share your food with the hungry and to provide the poor wanderer with shelter—when you see the naked,

to clothe them, and not to turn away from your own flesh and blood? Then your light will break forth like the dawn, and your healing will quickly appear; then your righteousness will go before you, and the glory of the Lord will be your rear guard. Then you will call, and the Lord will answer; you will cry for help, and he will say: Here am I. (Isaiah 58:6–9)

I then shared with them how the Lord had told me that He wanted a true fast from us and that He had said He would show His glory. I told them I believed that we would see lives given to Jesus for the first time and people healed. I prayed over everyone and we went out in four groups.

That day we bore witness to six people giving their lives to Jesus and many more encouraged in the gospel. We were thrilled. We returned to the house for some water, and when we got back a woman named Abigail approached me with a young girl. She said, "Sophie, I have seen the power of God today. And now, because I believe, I want you to pray for me and for this girl. We both have malaria." I prayed, "Jesus, we honor You as a God who is victorious over malaria. In Your name and to glorify Your name alone, we say, 'Be healed in Jesus's name!'"

Moments later, a grin spread across Abigail's face. She said that the migraine-like headache she had had moments before was gone. Later I got word that there was no longer a trace of malaria in Abigail's blood and that her platelet levels had returned to normal. The young girl had no more symptoms.

∽

As testimonies continued to pile up, encouraging me to walk out this precious calling to Zambia, a struggle began within me. I couldn't see it at the time, but I was doing what I could to keep Jesus out of it. The immeasurable grief that still consumed me and the constant ups and downs of everyday life had taken hold of my spirit, and I found it extremely difficult to remain steady. My prayer life, my attitude, my strength, and my emotions were bound to the events of each day, and my passion mixed with my anger at the things I was seeing (extreme poverty, abuse, disease, and injustice) was causing a great ferment deep inside of me. Without pressing into Jesus's heart, I kept throwing questions at Him. *How can this be?* I asked. *Kids in America play video games and ride in $150 car seats while children here starve and walk in bare feet.*

The slope was slippery, and before I knew it, I was pouring all of myself into ministry to avoid the conflict within me. My days began and ended with ministry. Every hour was consumed with trying to best spend myself on the people whom Jesus had sent me. I completely lost sight of what He was really looking for. I convinced myself that He wanted me to focus on meeting the needs of others, because if I let myself think anything different, I'd have to face not only the brokenness I could see but also the very real brokenness within me. And I didn't want to do that.

One night I sat in my little home on a scratchy, hot chair with my legs tucked underneath me. I hadn't bathed in six days, and at that point bathing didn't seem necessary. The night air was stiff and dry, and a bitter taste began to fill my mouth. I opened my Bible, hoping that God would reach down and relieve me of the bitterness and the grief that seemed to be growing in my heart.

"Jesus replied: 'Love the Lord your God with all your heart and with all your soul and with all your mind. This is the first and greatest commandment. And the second is like it: Love your neighbor as yourself'" (Matthew 22:37–39).

As I read this over and over, I heard the Holy Spirit whisper through the Scripture, "Sophie, love me. Love me with all of your heart. Love me with all of your soul and all of your mind. This is what I am looking for. This is what I made you for."

I was confused. I was giving every ounce of energy I had to what I thought He had called me to Zambia to do. But that wasn't the point. Deeply baffled, I asked, *It's not about ministry? It's not about all of these testimonies? It's not about all of this labor? It's not about me putting off my brokenness and pushing through? It's not about serving all of these precious people that You love? Isn't that why You brought me to Zambia?* In all gentleness I felt Him reminding me that everything was simply about loving Him. All He was after was my love. We can become only what we behold.

I pulled my legs out from underneath the weight of my body, and my heart began to throb. I was still so desperately far from loving Him. Though I knew I had genuinely surrendered my life and had chosen obedience, I realized I wasn't prioritizing loving Jesus first. I had made the mistake of letting grief and despair over what I was seeing dictate my priorities, making my first love serving Him. I was trying to ride to Him on the tide of ministry success and exciting testimonies. I had been doing good works to gain acceptance in His eyes, as if I could earn His love. I began to see that I was missing the point and therefore was missing everything.

The key was in what I was avoiding. Grappling with my brokenness and my unresolved grief was the very thing that could catapult me into a life of love. Blessed are the poor in spirit (Matthew 5:3).

∞

Over the next few months, my failures and frustrations continued to be brutally visible and nearly paralyzing. My passion to love Jesus first and to live out His teaching was real, but there was no visible evidence that my grief, brokenness, and perpetual stumbling were coming to a halt or even lessening. My life wasn't looking more like His, and this caused me great despair. Many days I felt a raw sense of hopelessness dulling the clarity of my mind, and I felt bitterness toward the growing shame within me. I despised my brokenness.

Throughout this season, I remembered and continued to read the words in Matthew 5:3–4, "Blessed are the poor in spirit, for theirs is the kingdom of heaven. Blessed are those who mourn, for they will be comforted." I wasn't entirely sure what this meant, but I asked the Lord for revelation specific to these two verses. Over time, I grew in the knowledge that I was blessed as I recognized my need for Him and as I mourned my depravity. I invited Jesus in and turned a corner by intentionally addressing my brokenness and my wanderings. I found freedom to be honest with Him about the fear and the shame in which I had been living. I cried out to Him for mercy, and though most of the time I didn't feel He heard me, I kept asking.

I battled to understand the blessing in seeing my brokenness and how to face it without letting it knock me to the ground or entrap me. Much of the time, I was lonely and scared, and it didn't help that I was also extremely weak physically. I had been working so hard and giving myself so fully to ministry that my body was not getting enough rest. At the five-month mark I had a near-death experience with a bacterial infection that led to septic shock, leaving me in a small hospital for several days. My life had been miraculously spared. The doctor informed me upon my discharge that had I arrived thirty minutes later, my organs would have completely shut down and I would have died. Looking back on the horror of the moments before I fell into a comatose state, I remember being brought to a place of peace where I was reciting Psalm 23 over and over as Jesus laid me in a field of green grass. The missionaries who rushed me to the hospital recall nothing of the sort since my groans and screams of agony were all that filled their ears.

I was absolutely thankful to find the sweet mercy of Jesus during my physical healing in the following weeks, but I was still engulfed in a sea of confusion over all the other surrounding realities. I couldn't believe how unhealthy my perspective had become and how far I had gone to avoid facing what was broken inside of me. In my weakness, I battled with the truth day and night. I kept wondering, *How can the poor in spirit be blessed? And how can life be all about loving You, Jesus? Did You really create me simply to love You?*

Day after day, I continued to press on with the small strength that I had. I found to my surprise that though my brokenness was always before me, it was not meant to crush me. Instead, my grief and my brokenness could be embraced as a bridge that allowed me to step into a place of poverty of spirit, where I could see my need and then be catapulted into the One whose love would bring me to life.

My call to Zambia had little to do with ministry. It had everything to do with learning to love a God who would use even my brokenness to draw me to Himself.

CHAPTER

You Say My Love Is Real

What I couldn't understand about my life in Zambia is how I could be filled with such deep, radiant joy and then, even hours later, collapse on my bed at night weeping. Dark nights seemed to escort in deep cries, and deep cries continued to expose deep wounds and confusion within me. Almost every night, despite utter exhaustion, I stayed up into the wee hours evaluating how great the need was all around me. My insides were in anguish as I questioned whether I was doing what Jesus wanted. The need seemed so dire, almost untouchable, and I wanted to spend myself. The process of learning to walk in love for Jesus first was difficult in a land where need was always before me. I had to learn what love looked like. I was in love with Jesus and with the people of Zambia, but I wasn't sure how best to live out that love.

Despite all I still had to learn, I was certain that my beloved Zambian sisters, mothers, and little ones were being blessed and that I was being blessed even more. I knew that I was seeing miracles and testimonies of salvation and redemption and that I was growing in love. I knew that I was seeing malaria bow to the name of Jesus and I knew that six years of a woman's hemorrhaging had to cease when Jesus heard us declare His name over it. I knew 168 souls could be saved in a single moment, and I knew an orphan's life could be changed forever because she had found a safe place where she could be fed and comforted after severe abuses. I knew that a fifteen-year-old, who had been raised in the church but had never known Jesus, would joyfully get on his knees and surrender, hands held high in the air, as the gospel was presented to him with power. I knew Jesus was alive in this land. I knew He had chosen me and had appointed me. But what was the point?

My heart struggled to be content as I wondered whether I was actually doing what Jesus had called me to do. I felt that I needed to give more or that my day-to-day life should look different. I despised my inescapable weakness, and I wanted my yes to feel stronger. I craved to have the Lord reveal a big and glorious plan for my life, in Zambia and wherever else He might take me. I longed for the Spirit to possess me completely and to feel His fire always. My deepest cry was to embody Jesus as I ministered each day—whether to hundreds or just one, simply to embody His faithfulness.

But contentedness was far from me.

I was broken. I was hungry. I was weak and young and lonely. I had stagnant and unresolved grief deep within me that I couldn't share with anyone at home, simply because I knew there were people waiting to say, "I told you so" or "Just come home. You've done enough. Jesus doesn't want your life to be so hard." I wasn't willing to accept either of those answers, so I resorted to isolation. Jesus, forever trustworthy and faithful, was the one I could confide in, and Jesus was kind enough to receive the tears that I brought to His feet daily. My tears and my sighing were not hidden from Him (Psalm 38:9).

On a dark, humid night in the middle of Zambia's rainy season, I walked through the hall of my home, dull and exhausted after a long day. Time had been passing slowly, and I struggled to balance what was happening on the ground with what Jesus was revealing to me each day. I woke up most mornings with dreams and visions of Jesus splitting the sky on His coming return. I heard Him whisper deep secrets of His heart to my soul. I would get caught up in gazing upon His beauty and then realize that it was a normal day and that I had monotonous operational tasks to accomplish. Morning after morning, He was drawing me deeper and deeper into Himself, and yet nothing about my earthly circumstances felt the least bit glorious.

I stumbled around the small kitchen, running my hand up and down the wall, trying to find the light switch. I was thankful that the power had returned, since it had been out for several hours. I opened the fridge to find a can of grape Fanta that I had saved as a treat from the day before. Something about the tingle that traveled down my throat revived me at the end of the day or at least energized me for a few moments. I made my way to the small, uncomfortable chair in the foyer and sat down. *Jesus, I love You. Come fellowship with me*, I asked silently.

Loneliness had plagued me since I moved to Zambia. Fellowship with other missionaries was rare, and I was unsure how to cultivate cross-cultural friendships. The narrow road seemed an impossible path, and I was constantly tempted to return to my earlier life. Everything in my flesh wanted to quit. I was utterly dependent on Jesus just to make it through each day. But although the truth was difficult to embrace, in the deepest part of me I knew with certainty that my days were within God's purposes. I would struggle, but nothing would be in vain.

Suddenly, I heard my phone ringing in the outside pocket of my little backpack. I stood up, walked across the room, and pulled it out to look at the screen. I didn't recognize the number, but I decided to answer the call anyway. I didn't know that when I hung up, I would feel the pain of a betrayal I had never seen coming. I wrote in my journal:

> Silent tears drip with no one on earth to notice, and I cry, "There is nowhere else for me." There is no greater peace than at Your feet, Jesus, nowhere else I can lay down everything. There is no other place to lay down my day, no other place to recognize that not in my strength but only in Yours am I found. There is no greater place than at Your feet to lay down my offense and to love You, O Jesus.

Silent prayers escape, and there is no one but You to hear, my Jesus. My spirit weeps, and I am desperately hurting. My flesh wants to pick up offense and self-pity, but I refuse. Pain and exhaustion belong to me, but I declare that I am free. The weight gets heavier. Oh come with Your peace. Days drag on longer. Oh, but just to be at Your feet. I can't leave. I won't leave. I belong at Your feet. Oh, take these tears. Take this weeping, and turn these tears to love. That's something only You can do. I ache from the deep to the shallow. Only You can heal me. Jesus, take these tears. Store them in an alabaster jar, and receive them like incense. Only You can see my mourning and count it as love. When I don't understand and still I turn to You, oh, find that I love You. Jesus, receive my adoration and my allegiance to You. Receive these tears as love.

Suffering more grief in my stifling loneliness was extremely difficult. Most days it was hard to get out of bed. I was lonely and ashamed. It was easier for me to believe the lies of the Enemy and easier to believe that what had been done and said was true. My heart was grieved, and yet each day Jesus was meeting me and responding to my cry. He was holding my tears, and somehow I knew He was receiving my love, weak as it was.

☌

The morning air was cool and fresh with only an ounce of humidity after the long, dark night. My spirit felt harsh and brutally misunderstood. Just past 4:30 a.m., I pulled myself out of bed, unrested and weary of my pillow.

I thrashed around in my room, quickly throwing things into a bag. I had decided to leave the compound and to take refuge in a few days of retreat. I desperately needed time away with Jesus, and I couldn't bear to be in the place where I was. I had to leave the flooded streets of the compound for a place where only Jesus could find me. I sought a place where I could lock myself in and not emerge until the Holy Spirit fell. I needed to know that even in my struggle, He was still beautiful and still called me His own.

I made it to the bus station an hour later and soon was en route to a little lodge several hours away. An exhausted thankfulness came over me, filling me with strong anticipation of what Jesus would do in the next few days. I longed for restoration and to authentically break before Him. His presence, I knew, would come like fire and would refine me. My beloved, with His all-consuming love, was after my heart. Instead of turning away from all that was hurting within me, I turned toward it. Desperation was my portion, and that was right where the Lord wanted me to be.

There is love to be known in every place of brokenness.

After a seven-hour ride, the bus driver opened the door and I filed out behind many others. I landed on the hard dirt road and waited for the conductor to signal that the baggage door had been opened. He gave me the classic Zambian raised eyebrow, and I collected my bag from the compartment. I jumped in a taxi and soon arrived at the small lodge, quaint and slightly romantic. The Holy Spirit spoke tenderly to me, calling me into His chambers, calling me to Himself.

∽

The wooden door squeaked as I opened it. I rejoiced in what I saw, and my spirit leapt within me. The concrete floor beneath me was cool, and the cement blocks lavished with thick lavender paint were alluring. A small bed in the corner, draped with a mosquito net, promised me rest. Between two stacks of small blocks and behind a wooden barrier sat a toilet, and a shower lay behind a thin curtain. I quickly placed my bag on the floor and removed my shoes. I shut the door behind me, and my feet began to dance.

Despite all that was aching in my depths, I twirled around like a ballerina, and my spirit delighted as one in her youth. A smile spread across my face and tears streamed down my cheeks. This small concrete room, secluded and quiet, became an immediate place of encounter, and Jesus was all I wanted.

I fell to my knees and stayed there for hours. Puddles of pain and love, confusion and grief, poured out on the cold, hard floor beneath me. My emotions were raw and unsanctified, unplanned and authentic, but I wasn't scared. I began to feel a sense of being safe with Him, not concerned that I needed to hide or to tame my bloodied being. I had never responded to pain with such urgency for God's presence, and I knew this was beautiful. As I poured myself out in the most candid and wildly confident way, I felt Him tenderly cradle me. I knew without a doubt that He was receiving all this as love. Though my brokenness was great, He saw me loving Him still.

My large sketchbook lay open before me, and my Sharpie pen sat in the crease of the seam. My Bible rested under my chin, and I poured myself over it again and again. Ink in the freshly marked margins smeared as slight tears trickled down my cheeks while Jesus unmasked more and more of me before Him. He peeled back layer after layer of shame and condemnation, desiring to reach the deepest wounds in my spirit. Tenderly He kept me in His presence, cradling me with His strong hands. He ran His fingers through my hair and His right hand caught my tears. I turned over onto my back, and with outstretched arms I cried, "Jesus! Come near. I'm so weak, but I love You. I love You."

And ever so quietly, my breathing stilled and I lifted myself into the small bed in the corner. In the quiet of this little concrete room, I felt whispers over my being, telling me that this was the way to love.

Though I couldn't understand through the lens of my brokenness and sin, I knew my tears weren't all Jesus had been receiving. I knew that He saw my heart and that despite what seemed like a season of perpetual suffering, He called my love real. As His presence gently overwhelmed my entire being, I whispered back, "You say my love is real."

The next three days were quiet and sweet. Jesus was kind to bring me to a place of retreat where I could courageously embrace my brokenness and see for myself that there was love to be found there. His voice tenderly led me through His Word, showing me again that my love was what He sought. Ever so kindly, He whispered over and over to me that He saw my love and that it moved His heart. My discontent began to melt away as my weary frame felt His affection for me. My questions about whether I was living out all He had for me, and my desires to do more and to be more, shriveled as I listened to Him. His love was my life. And my love was His delight.

Jesus began to uncover me and unpack my misconceptions about who He was. Even in my deepest cries and my perpetual brokenness He wasn't exhausted with me. He had never insisted that I come to Him in strength or in some grand discovered purpose, nor was He even hoping for this. He saw me turn to Him in my brokenness and confusion and called me courageously beautiful. He saw my tears and He saw my love. And without belittling my grief, He reminded me that I was made for love.

The sweetest gift I could ever step into was to live boldly, broken as I was, in the middle of His desire. It was grace to believe that He loved me wholly and that my weak little yes was real. My love for Him, which felt so faint and fragile, was real.

My heart began to grow in gratitude and poise. Contentedness crept back and quietly took up residence in my heart, which had been so cold for so long. Though my wounds took time to heal and my tears flowed for days, I found my heart singing truths that would lead me into greater depths of sobriety and thankfulness in the days to come. Over and over, when bearing the weight of my brokenness didn't feel brave or beautiful, I reminded myself of the Lord's delight in me. And ever so quietly, moment by moment, I learned to whisper over myself and back to Him, "You say my love is real."

CHAPTER

REMOVE ALL THAT HINDERS

I t's an interesting thing when everything that was once normal vanishes in an instant. But more than that, it's an extremely intense experience when the reality of the new normal wages war on what used to be. I have learned that old routines rarely raise the white flag of surrender easily.

Before moving to Zambia, my life wasn't necessarily easy, but it was good. I loved Jesus. My ministry efforts were bearing fruit. I was well known and was involved in my community. I had lots of friends and a family that lived an hour away. I was a collegiate athlete. I was provided for and my needs were met. I secretly dealt with long-lasting traumas and grievances, but they were hidden deep down, far from accessibility. For the most part, I could alleviate my everyday struggles or rely on others to help me do it. Though there was much pain in my life and in the lives of people around me, I was used to brokenness being made better or completely healed. And if that wasn't possible, I could easily find distractions to bring me false and temporary comfort.

The transition from my southwest-Michigan normal to my new Zambian-compound normal was tough. It was now normal to cry myself to sleep every night, to be fondled and grabbed by men throughout the day, and to encounter severely abused women and children. It was also normal to hear heinous sexual comments by drunken men and to be confronted even in simple conversation with the proposition "Want to make babies with me?" It was normal to have bruises and sore limbs from being dragged into an alleyway, to be threatened with stoning and being thrown in fire while fighting to rescue children, and to be harassed and followed by individuals with legions of unrestrained demons possessing them. It was normal to hold babies who had been dumped in sewers, to feed children whose bellies and bottoms were being eaten away by worms, and to listen to little girls replay the abusive events of the night prior.

I had barely dipped my toes in the water after arriving in Zambia when my old thoughts on normal were turned upside down. When I started to see the tragedies happening every day in my new home, I faced the reality that even though Jesus had sent me here, I couldn't do much to fix any of these problems. Even worse, there was little I could do even to alleviate the pain of these precious ones. This didn't sit well with me. I was used to solving problems or doing something to relieve them. I was used to seeing Jesus change people's lives with breakthroughs and healings. I wasn't used to the enormous amount of traumatic suffering I saw in Zambia and to the country's deep and widespread needs.

I was troubled at not seeing the magnitude begin to lessen. It seemed that for every plight I saw, my eyes were opened to ten more. Every day the depravity grew, and that frightened me. I wanted to see the brokenhearted set free and to have Jesus vindicate His innocent ones. I wasn't okay with the fact that the five minutes I might have with a child could be the only physical comfort that child would receive in an entire week. I struggled to relinquish control over these lives to Jesus. He had brought these children into my home but wouldn't make a way for them to stay. This became a huge issue in my view of Jesus, and it stung. On every level, this traumatic, horrendous, and beyond-description new normal stung.

Jesus was set on refining my spirit with searing heat. He knew that if He confronted me with the unrelenting plight of the brokenhearted, which I could do nothing about, I would be emptied and humble enough to ask Him to share His heart for the fatherless with me.

Though I didn't know it, this humility would launch me into a deeper understanding of my inheritance as one laboring with Him. And here, more than the failing attempts of one woman to take up the burden of all these children, was communion with Jesus, who will personally vindicate each one. Jesus will see to it that these children are redeemed and restored, even if I never do.

∽

One day after I had completed my primary responsibilities, I was prompted by the Holy Spirit to visit a crisis orphanage. I had been there only once before, and since then I had repeatedly asked Jesus for another opportunity to go. The heat of the February afternoon was stifling, and I felt Him stirring my heart. With the soles of my feet on the cool tile of my home, I rocked back and forth with my hands in the air as I cried out, "Holy Spirit, possess me!" I steadied my gaze and sobered my heart before Jesus, opening my heart to Him. Though I wasn't sure what it was, I knew something was happening in the spiritual realm.

I left my home and walked toward the taxi stand to catch a lift. Though sixty thousand kwacha (equivalent to twelve dollars) was a lot since financial support was slim, I felt an urgency to reach the orphanage more quickly than the hour and a half it would take me to walk there. I felt around in my purse, pulled out the money, and jumped into the taxi, which was parked up against a store's security gate. Though I had been outside only a few minutes, beads of sweat crowned my forehead and dampened my underarms. Sweat dripped behind my knees, and my skirt stuck to the back of my legs. A fuzzy Zambian radio program blasted in the background, and the breeze from the open window felt like a hot hair dryer blowing in my face. Flies buzzed violently around me, but my only thought was that in a short few minutes, a precious child would find refuge in my embrace.

I couldn't help but anticipate all that Jesus would do as I sought His heart for these children. I could almost hear Him whispering secrets over these little lives, stirring me to step into belief over their inheritances as sons and daughters of the Most High. I was prepared to fight for these innocent ones and to labor in intercession over them in the short moments that they rested in my arms. I declared under my breath that because Jesus made it clear in the Bible that visiting the orphan was true religion, I knew that more would happen during my time at the orphanage than would meet my eye.

I walked in and there she was, little Nakukenga. I could barely get my sandals off before one of the caregivers brought her over to me. As she wiggled beneath three blankets, I could start to make out her tiny frame. It was obvious just by her face, though, that malnourishment had left her entire body skeletal. Her body came to a rest as I drew her near. I looked down, gazing into her eyes. I couldn't help but stare at such beauty. I wrote in my journal later that night,

> Just over four pounds, she lies in my arms; a beauty she is. I cradle her close to my chest; the warmth of her tiny body captures me. In awe, I stare at her. Her ears and tiny nose leave me speechless.

She pulls her little fist close to her face, and she rubs her tired eyes. I've never seen something so precious. My hand supports her damp bottom. The smell of urine meets my nose as the most fragrant glory. I begin to pray.

> I am overcome with visions of her at age five, ten, even twenty: a prophetess and a woman of the Word, a woman whose perfume will pour out on Jesus alone.
>
> And then my eyes are opened to the most beautiful of all things: her lips tightly wrapped around her little bottle. "Like newborn babies, crave pure spiritual milk" (1 Peter 2:2)
>
> This is what we must become: weak, dependent, and hungry. This is the fragrance of the sweetest perfume.

I sat on the hard floor, lost in a dream of beholding Jesus's heart for this child. My hands, clammy from the heat, gently unwrapped little Nakukenga's body from the swaddle of blankets that padded her frame. Little by little, I pulled out her tiny limbs, allowing them to surface and to breathe. Slowly, I brought her to my chest where her delicate little bones could rest comfortably. I cringed as I moved her, nervous that any sudden movement of mine could break her in half. I had never held a baby so small, an infant nearly three months old, weighing barely four pounds. I couldn't take my eyes off of her. For a few hours, there we sat: Nakukenga and I, my world caught up in hers and her world resting in mine. Oh, how close Jesus comes to the lonely.

∞

The afternoon sun was making its way behind the trees as the hands of the clock reached 17:00 hours. Caregivers were scurrying around the room, showering and preparing to change shifts, and babies were lulled to sleep by the mundane routine. The smell of anti-fungal soaps and soiled cloth diapers filled my nostrils, and my stomach began to growl as I caught whiffs of steaming hot porridge. I hadn't eaten all day and I was hungry enough that even porridge was appetizing.

A young caregiver, who looked to be about my age, entered the room. I had seen her once before, and her demeanor seemed rather downcast this time. I couldn't remember her name, but as she ventured across the room and took off her shoes, I heard someone greet her, reminding me that her name was Musonda. If I remembered correctly, she had an incredibly beautiful smile, but I didn't think I would see it this evening. I began to pray, and for the next hour or so, I watched her move about the room, caring for the children, who were waiting to be fed. Compassion bled out of her, and I could tell something was heavy on her heart. Her hands were strong but so tender with each child she held to feed. Every movement she made was soft and quiet, and she fought hard to hold back tears. I maintained my quiet and inviting posture, hoping she would sit down. I continued praying.

The bottles of porridge cooled on the table for a few minutes, but soon another caregiver began distributing them. I stood up, made my way over to the table, grabbed Nakukenga's bottle, and then sat down in a strong rocking chair. I watched little Nakukenga as she worked hard to suck down the porridge, and I paced her feeding. As she neared the end of the meal, her eyes dulled and rolled back in exhaustion. She fell into a deep sleep, evidencing the weakness of her frame; Nakukenga barely had enough strength to eat. As I tapped the bottom of the bottle to get the last drops into Nakukenga's mouth, Musonda sat down right in front of me. I felt the slight weight of Nakukenga in my arms and the intense weight of whatever was on Musonda's heart. The day had finally reached its crescendo. I rose from the chair and sat down beside Musonda with Nakukenga sound asleep in my embrace.

"Musonda, I haven't seen you smile today. Are you okay?" I asked. After a few moments she looked into my eyes and sighed, saying, "I am very disturbed today." Without hesitation or any further prompting, sparing no details she told me that the day before, she had witnessed a newborn baby deliberately killed in the road under the weight of a minibus.

My mouth dropped and I caught a glimpse of her eyes before she quickly put her head down. I was silent. I had nothing to offer. My spirit instantly felt blasted with a monsoon of sheer grief, and no longer was my heart at peace with sweet Nakukenga on my chest. I took my hand off of her little bottom and placed it warmly on Musonda.

"I am so sorry, Musonda. I am so sorry you had to witness that," I managed to say a few moments later. "I am so, so sorry."

My spirit was grieved. Everything in me ached for Musonda, for what she witnessed was far too much for anyone to handle. I scooted a little closer to her and kept my arm outstretched, my hand softly rubbing her back. I couldn't believe what I had just heard. I couldn't handle it, and I despised the absolute helplessness that I felt.

We sat for probably thirty minutes with no more words, just quiet tears. Every few minutes I would look up and wait to make eye contact with Musonda, hoping that somehow this would comfort her, though shock was surely all she could feel. I was too stunned to move.

Precious Nakukenga slept as I cried. Her tiny body, which had felt weak and dull in my arms all day, was beginning to feel different. Her skeletal frame now seemed to be bursting with life, telling of a God who is alive. Her existence felt weighty to me, gently nudging my heart and my eyes to see redemption. It was impossible for my initial doubt to take root, because this tiny girl was alive, and only one thing could have sustained her. Where I had once felt little hope when I looked at Nakukenga, I now saw a miracle maker wholly sovereign over her existence.

The evening closed in and it was time to go. I placed Nakukenga in her crib and wrapped my arms once more around Musonda. There were no words to be spoken except one last "I'm so sorry." And with that, I quietly walked out.

In the wake of such a tragic story, I began to feel a potter inside of me, carving out a place for Himself to dwell and to share Himself with me. The knifelike pains that jabbed at my insides were the strong hands of my King making more room within me to behold His heart for the brokenhearted. Those strong hands were purging me and etching faces and images upon my heart that would cause me to tremble. He was set on one thing: removing all that hinders love.

I didn't know how to love Jesus in such helplessness and suffering. I didn't know how to worship Him with images of newborn babies exploding under the weight of minibus tires flooding my mind. I had no understanding of how to still lay my affections on Him and adore Him when such atrocities were happening. In those moments I didn't feel He was worthy to be worshiped. I was so offended and so undone by such horror that I doubted His goodness, His sovereignty, and His perfection. I didn't doubt that He was Lord, but I was hindered in loving Him. I couldn't look at His eyes and believe they were pure. I couldn't look at Him and see the world and believe there was no darkness in Him. I couldn't face such terrors and still believe He was faithful. I was in a place where I just couldn't.

As the weeks passed, a deep revelation of the first commandment continued to lead me forward. Knowing that I was made to love the Lord, I couldn't stop asking Him to remove anything hindering my love. And as easily as my wandering heart wanted to pick up offense again and again and to put up walls, I continued to invite Jesus to tear them down. I somehow kept offering Him full access to my heart, though I knew His hands would hurt. In those desperate moments of my heart's wanderings, He was looking for a companion in me, hoping I'd respond to His invitation to share in His suffering.

I desperately needed the Spirit to teach me to continually position my heart for worship. When I thought about Nakukenga, I could see the hand of a miracle maker, taking up the inheritance He died for. And in the wake of the tragedy that Musonda had shared with me, I slowly began to embrace the truth that Jesus was still worthy of my affections and of a life wasted on Him.

Over time, I asked Jesus if He would teach me to see every broken child (fatherless, orphaned, vulnerable, hurting, or lonely) as a miracle bursting with life. I decided that if He was willing to do this, I could worship Him freely the rest of my days. If the Spirit could let me in on the secret of seeing the brokenhearted as the closest to Jesus's heart, one with Him in His suffering, I could trust His sovereignty and faithfulness despite what any circumstance could render. If the Spirit would introduce me to the God of the impossible and train my eye to see His strategy for victory, I could run this race hard and long and unhindered in love.

In response to my request, I began to feel the warmth of the Lord's Spirit and the depth of His compassion. His heart was pure in calling me to abandon my offense at this story, because His character was dripping with humility. I knew He wasn't asking me to pretend this wasn't real and to worship a God of rainbows and unicorns. Instead, His authenticity gave me space to grieve and to stand in a room of confusion without becoming a prisoner there. His invitation for me to worship Him wasn't caught up in pride but from the knowledge that He is perfect King who gave everything for my freedom. His desire for my rejoicing wasn't to falsely pacify my grief but to release me from the shackles of confusion and to send me out in authority. His voice was full of promise and all-knowingness.

In retrospect I have come to understand that while I was seated on the floor of the orphanage, with many miracles in the cribs surrounding me, Jesus came and began to remove what was hindering love deep within me. His strong hands reached down into my heart and cradled me in my grief and my fear. His rod and His staff tenderly met me in a place of confusion and helplessness and, without disregarding my struggle, led me into His gracious presence. His pure eyes dove into my being where pride stood in the dark corner of my soul, and He so powerfully lifted the weight of my need to fix everything and be ok. His pursuit of my heart unveiled my helplessness so that I might meet Him in His sovereign power and love Him right there.

Jesus lovingly met me where I had been slain to the point of utter emptiness, and I realized my barrenness in this clash between heaven and hell could only, ever, find rest in Him. He gave me room to allow the hindrances of fear, confusion, pride, grief and helplessness to be exposed, and He promised to tend to them graciously in due time.

I felt love and adoration for His name increase again within me. And amid the magnitude of suffering in my new normal, I saw my white flag of surrender steadily rise.

Nothing would hinder my love.

CHAPTER

LEARNING TRAVAIL

Walking through the streets of shanty Zambian compounds does something to me. These compounds are slums, squalid, densely populated areas where poverty and disease are rampant. Whether I return home with mud between my toes because of the rains, with dust in every crevice during the dry season, or with soiled clothes because of a mixture of urine and diarrhea from all my little friends, something unexplainable happens. My heart is moved every time, and something in the depths of me yearns for Jesus. The pit of my belly feels linked to a realm of His kingdom, and I am hyper-aware of my surroundings.

The first compound I visited was just outside of Kafue. This small town is a beautiful place with glorious mountains and low valleys. The most gorgeous magenta flowers bloom in the desert sun, making even the dullest shades of brown come to life behind them. Rich, full clouds are stacked against the deep blue of endless sky, and every evening the sun sets with precious coral hues, pure and bold. Scenic Kafue screams of a divine artist's touch, one that faithfully brings forth beauty each day.

Within moments of setting foot on the soil that day in 2008, draped behind the fierce beauty of Kafue's landscape, I witnessed the torments of everyday life experienced by the people who called this compound home. The rigid ground caused me to cringe as it wore on shoeless feet. I saw malnourished children ply their way through sewage drains, chewing on plastic bags, and my heart burned in my chest. Filthy, unclothed babies crawling alone in the middle of the street caught me completely off guard; their desperate, empty eyes gazing lifelessly back at mine. The dramatic and contrasting reality that was present every day in Kafue devastated me, and I've never been the same.

June 14, 2008, changed me. I had never seen such incredible beauty and inconceivable depravity in the same place at the same time. But maybe I had been missing something. Maybe beauty could always be found in places long thought to be dark. And maybe beauty could still surface in places of utter darkness.

That is, if someone was willing to fight for it.

∞

I didn't know much about travailing prayer until sometime in the middle of 2010 while doing intense work on a case involving a child facing an unimaginable plight. I was gaining experience on the ground in Zambia and had been in the streets and the marketplaces of the country's most gruesome territories day after day. The weeks were long with only sporadic electricity and running water, and I finally got used to bathing with a single bottle of water. My endurance increased as walking long distances (sometimes with buckets and baskets on my head) became normal, though my feet still grew calloused and tired from the many miles.

I had finally begun to feel confident as I pursued child welfare cases. A fierce fire started to burn in me with the knowledge that I had been born to fight for justice. The core of my God-given personality combined with the circumstances of my life had given me a unique skill set that seemed particularly valuable in Zambia's darkest compounds. But I still needed to work through one thing. As a follower of Jesus I had to ask myself, *Who do you say that He is? And who will you say that He is in regard to the injustice that will inevitably endure in this nation and across the globe until His return?*

I knew that in giving my life to combat injustice, there would be plenty of opportunities to pick up offense toward Jesus and to question His goodness and sovereignty. But rather than letting the injustices of this life deem the gospel a lie, I knew there had to be a way to stand firm on the truth of His Word. Despite any decree that circumstances could render, His goodness would always bring forth justice. After all, justice is the foundation of His throne (Psalm 89:14).

I had to bind myself to this truth. It wasn't a question of whether I could remain true to what I believed. I needed a way to connect myself to the reality of His justice. I needed Him to lead me to a place where I could learn what this fight was truly about.

One night I was sitting in my room after what felt like an impossible day, and in the deepest part of my being, I felt the Holy Spirit showing me that I could pick up offense or pick up travail—but not both. (I didn't know what the word *travail* meant, but I wrote it down and saved it for the next time I visited the Internet café). Though I didn't fully understand, I felt that travail must somehow be opposite of taking offense. I sat quietly and continued to talk to Jesus, listening for His voice. I didn't hear Him, but after a time I decided that the opposite of picking up offense was somehow closely tied to willingness.

∽

Travail, as I have learned over the years, is intense. At its core, travail means pain. The word is often used to describe the suffering a woman endures while going through labor and birthing a child. Travail is also synonymous with anguish, distress, and exerting oneself. Judging by the dictionary definition, travail appears to be anything but pleasant or honorable. But an invitation to travail in prayer is one of the most intimate and beautiful places we can say yes to step into.

Travail is a place for freedom fighters, a posture of heart twinning passion and willingness.

One afternoon in late 2010, I was walking home through the compound where I lived, dialoguing with Jesus about my day. Drunken men directed profanities at me as I passed a tavern, but simultaneously my eyes fixed on three little girls playing in the dirt just a few feet in front of them. Their soiled dresses barely covered their bottoms, making it obvious that they wore no undergarments. My heart burned and adrenaline shot through my veins as I recalled that three days earlier a young child was severely raped in an alley nearby. A fire rose within me as I recalled another very complex sexual assault case in which three precious young girls confessed that they had agreed to give themselves to a man for a gift, which turned out to be a single lollipop for the three of them to share.

Hours earlier that day, I had cradled another child directly following her abuse. She wept in fear and confusion, shaking violently. I had endured the first of several threats on my life and had been grabbed and fondled just two days earlier. A hardly conscious woman had been to my home the midnight before with two of her children, reporting the abuse she was suffering at the hands of her husband. Her sweet daughter was blanketed in guilt and shame because she had failed to grab a pan from her father before he smashed it over his wife's head, knocking her out. The girl sat quietly in a corner while the woman's pain-stricken son sat numb beside her.

As I neared home, exhausted and heavy, tears began to fall from my eyes—first slowly with big, thick drops every few seconds and then quickly progressing to a much more intense ache than my body could contain. I barely made it through the gate and into my house where I doubled over with a deep groan. There were few words spoken in the following hours, otherwise it was only agonizing cries.

I managed to make it to my bedroom where the walls pressed in on me, creating an eerie and horrifying stillness. Though anyone else would have found the room completely normal, I feared it was seconds away from being ripped off its foundation and destroyed, taking me with it. This terrifying thought reminded me of when I was young and witnessed the dark and eerie moments of unnatural pause right before a tornado hit. These moments of eerie stillness felt exactly the same as those I recalled from my youth except that instead of following my parents' instruction to rush down to the basement where I would be safe, I felt an invitation from my Father to enter the storm and to seek Him in it.

The great deep of His justice was about to blow over.

The setting sun cast a gray and orange hue onto the glossy aqua of the walls, leaving the scene vague and dull. Smoke from burning trash in the alleyway just outside crept past the barred windows, sending thick toxins into the room. Like a tornado making a violent entrance, I threw my head into my pillow and screamed. Tense and coated in sweat, my body thrashed against the wall beside me. My insides felt ablaze with agonizing fire as if a razor blade were turning me inside out, and I was desperate for breath. My spirit wailed and I continued to weep. The Spirit of God was over me, entrenching me in the fire of His desire, and I realized something. He wanted justice more than I did. His heart bled for the innocent more than mine did. His anger at injustice and His deep compassion for these precious ones were stronger than mine. Travailing prayer was an opportunity He was gifting me. It was an invitation to bring my aching heart into the presence of a God whose heart aches more—an opportunity that couldn't be afforded to an offended heart.

In the midst of peril, I was contending for His scepter of justice. Instead of picking up offense and accusing Him for the horror experienced by these innocent people, I was connecting myself to the fire of His eyes, that burns with His desire to secure justice for each one (Psalm 140:12). Travail allowed me into the room where I could offer my deepest pleas on behalf of the innocent, all that God might in the end remind me of His final jurisdiction. Even if earthly circumstances did not yield the justice I was crying out for, still I could throw myself into His heart and His fierce desire, binding myself to the truth of His character.

He is the worker and the securer of all justice (Psalm 103:6).

He would see to it.

That night I recalled my initial experience in a Zambian compound, in Kafue. I remembered how vibrant those magenta flowers were, and I wondered *If those flowers could blossom from literal dust, what other beauty is waiting to surface?*

I began to see why I was so drawn to places known to be dark and only dark. I began to understand, again, why I had been called to carry the stories of the afflicted. Beauty is destined to rise from dust; that's who God is. The Creator inside of me had long ago begun pottering my heart with a fire to face injustice, but now He was tenderly leading me away from offense and into willingness. He wasn't promising an immediate breakthrough in the moments of our joint travail. Instead, He saw fit to let me anguish beside Him, knowing again His character, knowing again His flame-filled eyes, where injustice stands no chance.

Oh, that we might be willing.

> Your Spirit has fallen tonight. Jesus, I am Yours. How intensely incredible and intensely painful, but oh, what a place of union with You. I see Your eyes, and that changes everything. Come, King of heaven. Bring forth justice in this land.

PART 3

GAPING WOUNDS AND WAR

"The Spirit you received does not make you slaves, so that you live in fear again; rather, the Spirit you received brought about your adoption to sonship. And by him we cry, 'Abba, Father.' The Spirit himself testifies with our spirit that we are God's children. Now if we are children, then we are heirs- heirs of God and co-heirs with Christ, if indeed we share in his sufferings in order that we may also share in his glory."

—Romans 8:15–17

CHAPTER

CALLED A SATANIST

The day I said yes to Jesus for the first time was a sweet one. I was fourteen and staying at a Christian summer camp in southwest Michigan. In the evening I hiked up a hill where I laid myself down at the foot of a cross and wept in my brokenness and need for a Savior. I fumbled with a hammer as I drove a nail into the hard surface, and my spirit wept as I acknowledged that it was my sin that held Jesus on the cross more than two thousand years ago. That summer night with friends and camp counselors there to celebrate with me, I said yes to Jesus, which I am certain forever altered my eternity.

I returned home on a spiritual-summer-camp high, excited about my personal new-life resolution and with a checklist of Bible studies and "how to better honor your parents" tip sheets. I had new envelopes made to send my tithe to church, and I had a little evangelism card that went in my backpack so I could share Jesus with my friends on the bus and at school. It was such an exciting time with the whole world to personally gain because of my decision to follow Jesus. A community surrounded me in my decision, and I found great approval, satisfaction, and confidence on this new journey of being a better person and a

Christian. After all, those two things were synonymous to me and at that point, everything I could ever want for my life.

It was that cold night in June, almost exactly five years later that I said another yes to Jesus. In light of eternity, neither was weightier, but this yes was sober and driven by love. It felt different from the yeses I was saying each day to Jesus and different from the yes I had said back at summer camp. On the inside, it felt like the biggest yes I had ever said, mostly because it wasn't about me at all, though I didn't really know what I was saying yes to. As much as I hated to admit it, so much of my first five years following Jesus had been me-centered.

I knew that this decision would cause a commotion in my community and would probably pull me away from the familiar storehouse of self-affirmation and prosperity. I knew that Jesus was calling me to come and die and that He would lead me on a journey of persecution, homelessness, and intense suffering. And when I said this yes, appalling as it was, I knew that whatever pain came my way was incomparable to the surpassing worth of Jesus; my yes was for Him and for Him alone.

Jesus has never been interested in my yes to religion and my quest to be a better person with His help. He's always, only, ever been interested in my yes to pick up my cross, and to follow Him. And doing this, fixed on His eyes alone, is without a doubt the greatest honor of my life.

I was visited early by persecution. From the moment I opened my mouth about my decision to go to Zambia and to leave my life behind, intense accusation planted itself on my doorstep. Looking back, I still tremble thinking about those early days and about the heavy labor of keeping my head above the raging waters. Though I walk in freedom now, I will never forget the intensity of the rejection and the pain in that season.

Because of this early introduction to rejection and persecution, stepping onto the mission field felt freeing and vindicating. The moment I took my first deep breath of that thick Zambian air, sweet relief rushed over me. In my mind I believed that it was time for the storm to calm and for the waters to die down. It was time to plunge into Zambian life, coaxed by the hope that persecution would end and that time could only work in my favor. I thought that eventually Jesus would iron out all the wrinkles, dot all my i's, and cross all my t's and that I'd be well on my way to implementing perfectly strategized orphan advocacy and care and to seeing a revival break out in Zambia. That would vindicate me before my adversaries and would label me as an inspiration and a radical follower of Jesus, opening doors for my reacceptance. And maybe it would even pave the way for all the other decisions I would make in obedience to Jesus in the years to come.

If I'm honest, this quest sat on the throne in my life for quite some time, and when I started hearing apologies and receiving affirmation from loved ones back home, Jesus began to tear down what so sneakily had become another me-centered gospel that had taken root in my life. After more than a year and a half of serving wholeheartedly and loving genuinely, four words about me began to circulate throughout the Zambian compounds that caught me completely off guard. These four words destroyed everything I thought I had going for me and stripped me again of my self-centered theology.

"You are a satanist."

"A what?" I said as one of my dear Zambian mothers informed me of the accusation that was circulating in the compounds.

"They are saying that you are a satanist, Sophie. They say you are one of Satan's wives, and the blessings you are giving, they are curses. They think you worship Satan and the money you have, and the things you do are all curses. They can be nice to your face, but when you go they are talking as if you are a satanist."

"Are you serious?" I said, astonished and grief-stricken. "Really? Jesus, how can this be? No!" This accusation had come once before, early in 2010, but it was much different then. The people who had made it had been severely abusing a child who was taking refuge in my home, so it made complete sense to me. I wrote it off as their attempt to fabricate a story to undermine our efforts to rescue this child, and I was hardly phased by it.

But this time, singled out after being on the ground for more than a year and a half, those words lit my insides on fire and a prideful rage filled me. I thought, *How on earth can people even entertain that idea, let alone throw the accusation? How can anything I've ever done for these people be misinterpreted as evil and malicious? How can Jesus setting people free and healing them be misinterpreted as satanism?* My mind swirled like a tornado, bringing to the surface deep and intense experiences that I had been through since moving to Zambia.

How could a man who introduced himself to me as a lover of God and then begged me for sex escape accusation? How could my landlord, who wanted her property to "honor the Lord," steal hundreds of dollars from me and not be called a thief? How could these people praise me to my face and ask why I would leave beautiful and prosperous America to come to Zambia if they thought I was a Satanist? How could they keep coming to Bible studies and listening to the Word come out of my mouth and receive my teaching but then say that I worshiped Satan? How could people walk away from all the times when revival had taken root in hearts and many had been healed and even entertain the thought that I wasn't solely devoted to Jesus? How could 168 souls be saved in a single meeting if Jesus wasn't beckoning them through the Word I was preaching? How could this be?

The agony and distress in my spirit were multiplying, causing me to doubt. I looked up at my beloved Zambian mama, tears flooding my eyes, and said, "Mum, maybe I should just leave. I can't stay here like this. Even if my name is not spared, Jesus's name must be. I can't stay. Maybe everyone in America was right; I can't do this. Maybe my time here is up. I don't know if I can do this anymore."

I watched her heart sink to the floor, and then she looked at me firmly and said, "Sophie, you cannot leave. My daughter, you must stay. You must stay."

After a few moments of silence, I said fearfully, "Mum, you know I love Jesus and it is His name alone that I praise, right?"

"Yes," she said. And with enough certainty returning to her posture to comfort me and to assure me that everything would be okay, she wrapped her *chitenge* around her waist and got down on her knees beside me. And we worshiped Jesus right there on the stone floor of my home. Like never before, we worshiped Jesus with everything we had.

Later that day we had an afternoon prayer meeting at which I often taught. I was handing over leadership to some of the locals who had most intimately walked alongside me, and that was incredibly encouraging. This particular afternoon I was not teaching, and since my spirit was extremely fragile and exhausted, I was thankful. I was ready to be in the presence of Jesus and to stay there for a long time. I needed a word. I needed wisdom. I needed Him to speak boldly.

The Zambian sun was intense as I walked, cloaking me like an electric-heated blanket in a sauna. My cottonmouth gagged me, and I felt faint from dehydration. My eyes burned and the tight skin around them pulled at my face as I felt the residue from salty tears solidify in the sun. I must have looked terrible, but I knew that Jesus called me beautiful in that moment. My hunger was exposed to Him. My desperation and my increasing need for Him to shepherd me were not hidden from Him.

After an hour of walking, I stepped onto the sliver of cement block serving as a step and into the cool, dark building. It took a few moments for my eyes to adjust from the sun, but soon I saw the faces of so many women I loved. My heart throbbed with joy and relief at the sight of these precious mothers and sisters of mine, but then I remembered what was circulating in the compounds. The Enemy's lies swarmed around my heart like angry bees around a hive. *They think you are a satanist. The only way you can be free from this accusation is if you prove to them that you are not. You have to take the issue into your own hands. You must ask them if, after what Jesus has done, He would allow you to be called a satanist? You must ask them, "Why would you bother to worship Him if everyone thinks you worship me?"* I hesitated as I greeted the women one by one around the circle, as is traditional in Zambia, and I wanted to cry. I wanted to sob. But what I really wanted was for someone to hold me.

As usual, we began our meeting with worship and prayer, and my heart quickly melted before the throne. I am convinced to this day that no Zambian has ever seen me in as much of a mess as these women did. I was undignified. I was shameless in my weeping and I gave no thought to what they were thinking as I broke. Soon many women were weeping, and from the outside of the church, bystanders probably thought a funeral was taking place. The volume and the agony increased, but so did the unity. I heard the Spirit speak to the depths of my being, reminding me that it was time to pick up my cross.

After what seemed like twenty minutes but was nearly four hours, the heaviness that filled the room began to lighten. All of us women, filthy and exhausted from weeping on the floor, finally stood together and proceeded to the wooden pews. As we carried our crosses with somber hearts, I knew Jesus would keep speaking. I knew He would speak to us in such a way that all of the desperate hearts in the room would be restored when we left. And the most beautiful part was that none of us was in any hurry. He was our priority.

"I would like to ask our teacher if she would please read for us the Scripture. It is Luke 21," she said in a humble voice.

"Sure. Beginning in what verse?" I asked, slightly agitated that she had called me the teacher when obviously I was not teaching.

"Luke chapter 21, verse 14 through verse 19." And so I began to read. "But make up your mind not to worry beforehand how you will defend yourselves. For I will give you words and wisdom that none of your adversaries will be able to resist or contradict. You will be betrayed even by parents, brothers, sisters, relatives and friends, and they will put some of you to death. Everyone will hate you because of me. But not a hair of your head will perish. Stand firm, and you will win life."

We sat quietly for a moment and I reread the passage in my head. As I took in each word, I felt a numbing sensation spread through my body. I was amazed at this word directly from Jesus to His disciples, preparing them for persecution. In the quiet of my heart I questioned Jesus in awe. *Did You really just speak so directly and pinpoint the deepest cry of my heart at this moment and lovingly wrap Your promise around every wound of mine? Are You really going to come right now and with this word set my heart free of all the accusations against me?* And with a subtle glance across the benches, the woman teaching looked at me, not knowing my awe, and said, "Yes, Sophie. He is."

With that reassurance, which only Jesus could have so beautifully orchestrated, I stood up and walked out. Jesus was beckoning me into the secret place where I could be alone with Him, and I couldn't resist. From that point on, the words in Luke 21 went everywhere with me and revolutionized my innermost thoughts. The simple and piercing command to make up my mind not to worry beforehand raised the bar of faith in my inner being. This Scripture passage exposed the lies and the doubt in me, which had been yielding only fear and pride, and caused me to cast myself into Jesus's desire for me. Every day I realized more and more how desperately frail my faith was and how hopeless my cause would be if I didn't choose at each moment to throw myself into the victory of the cross. I finally started to see that because Jesus's pursuit is relentless, no betrayal or accusation by man could have any authority over me. I was invited to make up my mind not to worry beforehand how to handle false accusation and instead to free-fall into faith.

Matthew gives an account of John the Baptist and Jesus receiving false accusations against them. As the months passed and talk of me being a satanist failed to diminish, this passage hugely encouraged me and ushered in an exciting revelation that continues to fuel my love for Jesus. It is written: "For John came neither eating nor drinking, and they say, 'He has a demon.' The Son of Man came eating and drinking, and they say, 'Here is a glutton and a drunkard, a friend of tax collectors and sinners.' But wisdom is proved right by her actions" (Matthew 11:18–19).

As I meditated on this over and over, I thought, *Jesus, our Messiah, was labeled a glutton and a drunkard. John the Baptist, a man yoked to Jesus, was regarded as demon-possessed. What, then, can it matter if I, tiny Sophie, am called a satanist?* And one day, at the break of dawn, just as the sun shone through the iron bars over my window, I came to an understanding that would forever remind me to press on, allowing even accusation to push me foreword. I wrote in my journal,

> Jesus, I think I have just caught wind of what You are doing. I'm starting to get it. I'm in awe that You would offer me the opportunity to be so falsely labeled, to fellowship with You in accusation. Jesus, I'm not worried about this satanist thing anymore, because I am seeing that Your glory is wrapped up in all this.
>
> Mama said to me the other day, "They are not understanding you. They have seen you give the shoes on your feet to someone who doesn't have any and walk home with none even though you have money to buy yourself shoes in the market. And they have seen you drawing water and staying in Zambia for so long when they know you are coming from America."
>
> Jesus, not that I'm special at all, but maybe no one in this place has ever seen such a thing. Maybe it's just that not one of these people has seen someone who claims to be a Christian live the way I live and do the things I do. Maybe they can't understand why I would say yes to You when You ask me to love them so selflessly and to lay down my life to sit with them in their suffering. Maybe it's just that these precious people can't understand how my motive could be pure, how I could leave my American freedom to eat with them in the dirt. Maybe they can't understand me when I say that You have brought me here and that I truly am more blessed than they and ever so thankful.
>
> Jesus, it must be that they are offended that I would speak at an orphan's funeral when no one else noticed that he died, not even his family. They must not like that I prioritize caring for the lowliest, whom even much of the Zambian church has rejected. And I'm sure now that they can't understand why I refuse their offerings when You heal them or touch their lives in response to my prayers.

They can't understand why I would walk when I can pay for transport. They can't understand why I would endure all that I go through as a young white woman in this place when I could just leave. They can't understand that I would choose to live in a compound, knowing that it means walking to fetch my water and having electricity only some of the time. They can't understand. And even though many of them are believers, maybe they've just never seen the Gospel on display in this way.

And because they've never seen anything like it, they can only assume it must be the opposite. They can only assume that I am hoarding satanic wealth and binging on evil rewards. They can only assume that everything I do is motivated by an appetite for bloodshed when in actuality, everything I do is because of the blood You shed. It's You. And it's Your offense that offends them.

Jesus, You are so offensive, and I love You for it. Let me be like You. My desire to be like You exceeds my desire to be labeled by the crowds as one who follows You. For it's before Your eyes alone that I live, and You know I follow You.

The accusations that I was a satanist continued over the next few years. Speculation continued, particularly due to my increasing involvement with women and children in intensely traumatic and dangerous situations. As time went on, these situations yielded polarized stances in the community; some increased their accusations while others grew in confidence over my allegiance to Jesus. Though it was difficult to remain upright in heart and untainted by the opinions of others, I set my mind to walking in obedience to Jesus alone.

I quickly found that it was exhausting to be bound by fear, so I learned to release it. I knew that Jesus wanted me to love those who were falsely accusing me, and I knew that love had to look like something. Therefore I could let nothing hinder me from showing mercy and being grounded in true, authentic love. This meant that my desire to be like Jesus had to exceed my desire to be labeled by the masses as one who does. Love looked like laying everything down and looking right at Jesus.

Jesus let no accusation hinder Him. He let no misunderstanding of who He was distract Him from pressing on. His endurance proved that He was a man destined to wage war, and He was unconcerned about false accusations against Him. He is the greatest offense in all history, and He invites me to get out of the boat, to walk on the water, and to follow Him. And if I bear a false label for the rest of my life, so be it as long as it's His name that goes forth in and through my life.

CHAPTER 10

THE SACRED IN-BETWEEN

Simple acts of marvelous love change the world. Love, outlandishly displayed, always yields a harvest of revival. Intentional, genuine time spent with people makes a difference. Quiet, focused wholeheartedness toward Jesus and toward people moves the heart of our God. This is what I was learning.

Life in Zambia continued to wear on me, and I was struggling to keep up with the emotional load of everyday happenings. I was always seeing tragedy, my heart was consistently heavy, and my mind was unable to process all that was going on around me. I was growing increasingly exhausted by the day, and balancing my physical needs with my desire to stay up deep into the night with Jesus was hard. During the small periods of sleep I was getting, I was always waiting for the sound of abused women and children banging on the gate in the dark hours of the night. To this day, there is no feeling I remember more clearly than the one of the soles of my feet hitting the cold cement each time I jumped up, unaware of the severity of what I was about to see. The knowledge that this was what I was made to do was consistently paired with moments of terrible fear as I wondered how bad things were for the child who would soon be in my embrace.

During this time my night guard, Lubasi, was also getting used to sleepless nights and knocks on the gate. I regularly reminded him, "If it is a woman or children, let them in. Please let them in quickly without questioning them since they are probably in real danger." Some nights I gave Lubasi the names of women and children whom I knew were in peril, asking him to be extra attentive because they would probably be coming that night. And every evening as I gave him this instruction, I saw in his spirit a quiet compassion and a sense of pride and accomplishment. He was a gatekeeper for a house of the Lord. Lubasi, a broken and extremely impoverished man, was finding worth and purpose in Jesus, potentially for the first time. Looking at my life from a distance, it is obvious that purpose, direction, and favor were being poured out in abundance. That was amazing, but I kept getting more tired, and the mess around me kept getting messier. I loved it and I hated it and everything in between.

This concept of *in between* started to grip me in my secret time with Jesus. I started studying the topic of intercession (standing and petitioning in the in-between), and the Old Testament book of Joel had caught my eye and much of my attention. I considered the weight of every in-between (whether it be a long season, a short time, a stance, or a posture of heart), and I was moved to pursue an understanding of its importance. Having discovered the gift of travailing prayer, I set out in pursuit of deeper understanding. I knew at the most basic level that Jesus created the space in between and that in many cases that is the place He is after. It is a place of great worth and eternal significance.

Over and over I asked myself, *Is creation the climax of this story? Is our salvation and entering the holy city the sole crescendo? Or is it what is done in the in-between that makes God's creation and our consummation with Him an epic and glorious story of perfect, unfailing redemption?* With the brutal realities of broken women and children at the forefront of my mind, I repeatedly said to Jesus, "So if it doesn't matter what happens in between creation and salvation, then none of the pain that these precious children are enduring means anything. That means there can be no hope for them in this life, and I have no task here?" I cried and I longed for understanding. The depths of my spirit ached for the gap—that sacred space in between—and I wanted to move the heart of God in such a way as to call down the revelation that I so desired.

⚭

I found myself outside one afternoon seated on a small plastic chair under a mango tree among a group of beautiful children. I had gone to visit a precious girl named Mapalo who was traumatically malnourished and terribly weak after a near-death bout with malaria. As I held this sweet, tiny miracle in my arms, she quickly fell asleep. Her head met the pillow of my breast and her breathing steadied. She rested and I prayed. I whispered God's promises over her heart and spoke life over her.

After a few moments I caught sight of another little girl seated about ten feet in front of me. She was limp and unable to move from a filthy mat on the ground. Deep burns covered two-thirds of her body, all untreated and exposed. Swarms of flies surrounded her, worsening the infection, and she moaned in pain. Unable to shut her eyes and with no strength to swat away the flies, she looked straight at me. When our eyes met, compassion coursed through my veins.

Her name was Chisala, but everyone called her Ambuye, meaning "grandmother." Everyone began calling her that after her grandmother (the only family she had left) died and she would cry out day and night, "Ambuye! Ambuye!" Every day others mocked her in her sorrow, making a joke of her distress. And any time she cried they would yell, "Ambuye! Stop crying!" No one seemed to care that the name they called her was a reminder of what she desperately ached to have back, her loving grandma.

I watched her. With feces seeping from her soiled pants, more and more flies swarmed over her; she was beautiful. The stench she sat in burned my nose as I laid Mapalo down and made my way toward her, the thick mass of flies growing with the commotion of my movement. One of the ladies from the home abruptly yelled, "No, don't touch that one! I'm coming! I'm coming." I stepped back, honoring her command, but felt the weight of Chisala's plight intensify in my innermost being. The lady, whoever she was, swung her arm down and picked up Chisala by her elbow, carrying her into the little brick home like a smelly garbage bag, dangled off to the side so she wouldn't have to touch such filth. I couldn't help thinking of how Chisala was named in her distress and consistently taunted by her deepest cry. As I watched her being carried into the home, I realized that she was the lowliest of the lowly—easily the leper of all lepers. About five years old, she personified hopelessness, untaught of her worth or the promise of her coming healing.

I watched as the last shadow of her disappeared into the home. Her big dark eyes, still covered by flies, locked with mine, and the weight of evil hit me square in the face. I felt the atrociousness of sin as I understood that the Enemy delights in sending flies to eat at our eyes and enjoys naming us in our despair. He laughs at us as he taunts us, and he enjoys robbing us of the ability to see. The Enemy doesn't want us to see the sacred importance of the space in between our brokenness and our redemption, so he carries us out like the trash away from the One who sees us clearly.

I didn't see Chisala anymore that day, but I went home with her eyes in my mind. Anytime I thought of her, I was reminded of the in-between space I had been grappling with. I thought about Chisala, once safe and cared for by her grandmother, and I wondered what had happened. I cringed as I thought about her burns, the physical pain that bound her, and I broke as I considered her hopelessness. I meditated on Jesus's heart for her, and I knew that this suffering didn't come to her from His hand, but I couldn't understand. I wept and I begged Jesus again to give me revelation and to commission me. All through the night, I tossed and turned, wailing into my pillow, "What can I do? Now that I've seen her, Jesus, what can I do?"

The morning brought no answers, only silence and another child who would change me and cause me to grapple with the in-between.

ᕕᕗ

Her name was Taonga. She was four, and she was my friend. She was feisty and always filthy. She usually had snot dripping down her nose and feces smeared on her. What I loved most about Taonga was that every time she saw me she ran toward me, unashamed. She threw her arms wide open, and her little bowed legs trotted across the dirt until she found my arms. She usually let out a squeal that lasted from the second she saw me until the moment of our embrace, and her smile was wide. Her eyes were always bloodshot, and they screamed of her longing for love. She was sweet, she was a fighter, and she was hungry.

Nearly every day I had been leaving my house in the morning to visit Taonga. A few weeks before I had noticed a relatively large burn on the underside of her arm. The burn didn't seem too serious when I initially saw it, but in the last few days I had seen the wound grow considerably, and it was not healing. The wound needed consistent attention, and I had taken the responsibility of providing it.

On this particular morning, I struggled emotionally as I got ready to leave the house. I argued with Jesus over the reality of my pride, wondering whether the few minutes I'd spend with Taonga that morning were enough. I questioned whether properly cleaning and applying topical treatments to her wound was sufficient. I knew it would bring more healing to her body, but I selfishly grappled with the question of whether this was enough to make my day worth it. It horrified me to think I was so prideful, but that was the truth. I was wrestling with Jesus again, and He was after my pride.

I stepped outside of my gate and locked it behind me. In my bag I carried a variety of first aid supplies from which I would choose when I arrived. I walked down the dusty streets and made my way into the heart of the compound. Two minutes later, the shrieking began and the children bolted toward me. A little girl named Chipo led the pack, with Njovu, Kondwani, Chisenge, Sarah, and Bupe following. Their giggles and open arms blessed me, but I noticed that Taonga was missing from the stampede. After a glorious greeting full of squeals and hugs, I made my way up to the two-room flat where four families lived. There I found Taonga, sleeping on the hard ground. I turned the corner and peeked at the vegetable stand set up outside the house, looking for an auntie or any other adult, but no one was there. A six-year-old was in charge. I asked the other children where their aunties were, and not one of them knew.

I bent down and began playing with some of the kids, hoping that Taonga's aunt would soon return. My heart broke as I contemplated the danger these children faced simply in being left alone, and I felt a holy anger rise in me at the injustice of their plight. Taonga lay face down in the dust, hurting and alone. I thought, *And somehow she is supposed to know she is worth something? Somehow she is supposed to grow and to know the hope of her heavenly Father? Somehow she is supposed to learn that she is a priority and that she has a Father who cares about her every move?* With her lowly body sunk in the filthy terrain, I questioned how she would ever encounter these truths. I searched for something to convince me that she would someday be able to believe that she was worthy of love, and I heard the Holy Spirit whisper to my heart that even though twenty minutes wasn't a long time, it was still an opportunity to show her this. We cannot underestimate what He is able to do.

I set my bag down beside her and quietly lowered myself. I placed one hand gently on her back, wrapped the other around her body, and lifted her into my lap. She didn't wake, and her breathing didn't skip a beat. I held her closely and began to pray. As I prayed, I lifted her arm to check on her burn. The wound was growing and the infection had worsened considerably.

I felt around in my bag to find the right remedies. I quietly repeated, "Taonga, it's me, Auntie Sophie," and her eyes began to open. I stroked her face and held her near to my chest, and I kept whispering, "Auntie Sophie is here. Sweet girl, Auntie Sophie is here."

I took a large bottle of water out of my bag and steadily poured it over her arm. Though Taonga flinched at first, her arm remained relaxed, graced by the care and the promise of healing. The cool, clear water turned deep brown as it fell to the ground, rinsing out the bloody buildup that had been unable to fully clot. Several shards of charcoal flooded out under the slight pressure of the water, and visible to the eye was a deep red layer of flesh that was hoarding flies. The larvae had taken root deep in Taonga's arm, and nothing would heal without first removing them. Again, I held a child who was being eaten at by flies. The injustice, even just in her physical reality, was enough to double me over.

I sat for what seemed like an hour (but was just twenty minutes) cleaning out the deep infection. I cringed each time her little frame tensed, knowing that her silent tears didn't reflect her excruciating pain. My heart broke over and over.

As I finished cleaning her wound and began applying a series of creams and antibiotic ointments, I prayed desperately for this child. I bandaged her arm with thick gauze padding, and I prayed that Jesus would envelop her and seal her in healing. I prayed specifically that when her aunt came back, she would not remove the bandaging and that I would return the next day to find the wound miraculously healed. As I placed the last piece of tape to hold down the dressing, Taonga placed her other arm around my neck. She sighed deeply and shut her eyes, big tears escaping from either side. Though she was crying, her heart had stilled and she felt safe, wrapped up in the promise of healing.

She could rest now because someone had come for her.

And I stayed there for a little while longer.

∞

The small but enormously significant lives of Chisala and Taonga wrecked me. Their painful wounds and devastating situations pointed to what Jesus was teaching me in the book of Joel—the sacred in-between. Though the plights of these two precious children deeply grieved my spirit, they also provoked me and ended up catalyzing a greater understanding in the depths of me.

> Let the priests, who minister before the Lord, weep between the portico and the altar. Let them say, 'Spare your people, Lord. Do not make your inheritance an object of scorn, a byword among the nations. Why should they say among the peoples, "Where is their God?"' Then the Lord was jealous for his land and took pity on his people. The Lord replied to them: 'I am sending you grain, new wine and olive oil, enough to

satisfy you fully; never again will I make you an object of scorn to the nations' (Joel 2:17–19).

This passage speaks clearly of the role of those who minister unto the Lord: the job at hand is to weep. It is extremely easy to weep when dealing with children as impoverished and as broken as Chisala and Taonga (just the sight of them moves even the least compassionate person), but Jesus is looking for a more intentional cry. He is not looking for a cry charged by emotions alone. Jesus strategically directs us to the place where we are to weep—between the portico and the altar, the in-between.

If we look at the two places mentioned in this passage, we have access to an incredible amount of wisdom. A portico is an entrance, a doorway, or an entryway. It is like a porch. An altar is a platform, an elevated place, or a stand. With this simple knowledge, the Scripture passage can be understood like this: Let the priests, who minister before the Lord, weep between the entrance, doorway, or entryway and the platform, elevated place, or stand. Taking this one step further and using our brokenness as the starting point, this passage says, "Let the priests, who minister before the Lord, weep between the place of pain and the place of eternal healing." Between the entrance and the upper room, there is a gap of intercession. In that gap, in that in-between place, we find a sacred purpose of utmost importance. It is what we do there that matters. And the passage tells us to weep because as we see later in the book of Joel, weeping in this sacred space tugs on the heart of a jealous God and yields an outpouring of the Holy Spirit.

> And afterward, I will pour out my Spirit on all people. Your sons and daughters will prophesy, your old men will dream dreams, your young men will see visions. Even on my servants, both men and women, I will pour out my Spirit in those days. I will show wonders in the Heavens and on the earth, blood and fire and billows of smoke. The sun will be turned to darkness and the moon to blood before the coming of the great and dreadful day of the Lord. And everyone

who calls on the name of the Lord will be saved; for on
Mount Zion and in Jerusalem there will be deliverance.
(Joel 2:28–32)

In light of Chisala and Taonga, I began to see that as one
commissioned to allow my life to minister unto the heart of God I had
an incredible opportunity not only to accept but to seize and to embrace
the hard, unknown, and almost always dreadful in-between space. I
realized that I could do this because this passage in Joel told me that as
an intercessor, my cries tug on the heart of a jealous God who is full of
love and compassion. My weeping, between the unhealed wounds of
this life and the eternal healing that awaits us in Christ, is sacred and
purposed to yield harvest.

When all I could see was infection but all I chose to declare was
healing, that's where I began to tap into the grace of co-laboring with
Jesus. Much like travailing in prayer, the in-between is a sacred gift of
intimacy with Jesus.

I returned home after that hour with Taonga and collapsed onto
my bed. I pulled the mess of blankets over my head and buried my
face in my pillow. I wept and I ached, the burden seemingly too much
to bear. When I closed my eyes, all I could see was that sweet girl,
marked by pain, and yet my spirit was prompted to declare otherwise.
As I wept in that all-too-frequent agony, my spirit said it was time to
align my declarations with what Jesus accomplished on the cross. My
spirit insisted that though my eyes might not see an end to injustice and
Taonga healed, the end of the story had already been written. My spirit
required me to wage war against Taonga's plight by declaring over it
the victory of the cross. The depths of my being demanded that I take
my place between the portico and the altar and, on Taonga's behalf, tug
at the heart of our jealous God, who would send new grain and new
wine. My spirit persisted with the revelation that although pain and
wounds too deep to heal presently marked Taonga and Chisala, and

even physically they were being eaten at and destroyed, they were also marked by an eternal promise of healing and redemption.

The revelation of my commission to stand unwavering in the in-between changed my outlook on ministry, and I understood my weeping would tug on Jesus's jealous heart, beckoning Him to spare His beloved ones. Where many people find the in-between places and seasons in this life unbearable, I began to come alive in the beauty of this gap. And then, just as I read it in Joel 2:32, I heard Him say, "There will be deliverance."

11

CHAPTER

SOUGHT AFTER

How long, Lord, must I call for help, but you do not listen? Or cry out to you, "Violence!" but you do not save? Why do you make me look at injustice? Why do you tolerate wrongdoing? Destruction and violence are before me; there is strife, and conflict abounds. Therefore the law is paralyzed, and justice never prevails. The wicked hem in the righteous, so that justice is perverted. The Lord's answer: "Look at the nations and watch—and be utterly amazed. For I am going to do something in your days that you would not believe, even if you were told."

—Habakkuk 1:2–5

Unrestrained adrenaline surged through my body as I kicked up dust with the speed of my stride. My body swelled with the instinct to fight, and not even a raging bull could have stopped me. My vision narrowed as blood rushed to my face, and my heart thundered in my chest. I was focused and unstoppable—ever aware of the precise alignment of this moment and the call Jesus had placed on my life. Anger steamed out of my ears and nose, and fury propelled my pace. My weak frame now felt intensely strong and stable, and nothing could batter me. Nothing could instigate fear in me, and any attempt to destroy my appetite for justice would fail. I was ready for war.

The sweat between the soles of my feet and the plastic of my shoes caused difficulty in my gait, but it only fueled me more. Every little sign of weakness or discomfort only sent more anger and fight through my veins. My eyes were fixed ahead, my heart pounding. The battle was raging.

I made my way through the compound, the June winds blowing strong. I was coated in filth with a chalk-like, gritty film over my teeth. My nose itched and I could feel the buildup of dirt and grime inside my nostrils. My fingers swelled and I squinted in an attempt to avoid the dust. Small twisters emerged from bare ground, and whirlwinds collided in the open streets and tiny alleyways. The deep-gray sky seemed to hover over me, and the thick clouds seemed nearer than ever. Darkness was pressing.

"Jesus, I'm here, ready to be used. I am crying 'glory' as I worship You in turmoil. This is so intense, so dangerous, but I was made for this. Oh, that she might know she is worth it, worth every tear shed, every agony endured for the sake of her rescue and redemption. All is nothing in light of eternity. She is beautiful, and justice is in Your heart for her. Jesus, use me. I'm here, my life laid down, all of me for all of You. Use this adrenaline. Use this passion. Use me to embody Your faithfulness to this precious one."

I cried out loud as I made my way through the dusty streets. The words He was whispering to me solidified my purpose, and my brisk pace steadied as I approached the gate. My insides turned violently as I reached out to knock, and I stepped back as the guard opened the small frame, just large enough for a hand to pass through. "I am here for a meeting with the one in charge, sir." Without asking questions, he opened the gate for me and I quietly stepped through. My demeanor shifted dramatically as I felt the Holy Spirit calm my rage and usher me into sobriety and meekness. I understood that there was a harvest now and that today was crucial to this precious child's rescue but that this war would be won only with poise, endurance, and unrelenting pursuit. This was how Jesus would show Himself as steady, unstoppable, and unrelenting.

I cautiously entered the small office.

I met this precious girl in January 2010. Another woman and I had returned from church one day to find a woman and two children outside the gate to the service center, so we let them in. The children, both girls, one eleven years old and the other thirteen, were energetic and seemed excited to be welcomed into the home. Both spoke English, though one was dramatically more fluent than the other, and both had a sparkle in their eyes.

The younger one stood out immediately. Her smile was huge and beautiful, and her beauty was striking. She was tiny and her hair was short. She wore a faded pink tank top that barely covered her midriff, and her shoulder and arm muscles were extremely toned. She had the youthful delight of an eleven-year-old, but something in her eyes screamed a different story. Her maturity caught my attention, and I later wrote,

> She sits before me, and she is full of joy. I ask her what she likes to do, and she replies, "I like to share the Word of God."
>
> She's eleven. She begins reciting Scripture. Whole passages. I am humbled.
>
> With her eyes focused into the depths of my own and in clear English she says, "The Lord is my shepherd, I shall not be wanting. He makes me lie down in green pastures, he leads me beside quiet waters" (Psalm 23).
>
> My heart is overwhelmed as I watch and listen. The Lord is my shepherd. I shall not want. He has made me lie down in green

pastures, and He has led me beside still waters. He has. I'm here. Green pastures and still water.

An eleven-year-old spoke the Word of God boldly to me today.

And some call me the missionary. Bless her.

Over the next few months, the plight of this child ruined me, and she quickly became what seemed to be the entire reason for my presence in Zambia. Day after day as she shared horrific details of her story, I felt shattered and helpless. Her insidiously abusive situation overwhelmed me, and I was consumed with fear for her. My efforts, combined with those of another woman, seemed inadequate, though we faced danger in associating with this child and intervening in her unceasing traumas. A double orphan, having lost both parents, she had been passed from abusive household to abusive household and was subject to witchcraft and to demonic strongholds. Her history pressed hard into my heart. I knew her situation was not about me, but I thought I would never heal from seeing the wounds she suffered. I couldn't imagine how she was still alive, how she could find it in her to smile, and how she would ever heal. I couldn't understand how she could walk on legs that were once so horribly beaten. I couldn't fathom how she clung to Jesus. What had He done for her to demonstrate His faithfulness and to justify her pure and undistracted allegiance to Him?

"He brought you to Zambia for me," she would always say.

"They are becoming good people, Auntie," she whispered in my ear time after time. The cyclical abuse this child suffered was all too familiar to me. I pulled her close to my chest and she cried. I told her how incredible she was. I told her how proud I was of her and how brave a girl she was. I emphasized that Jesus had a plan and that He would bring it to completion (though I struggled to believe this most of the time). I told her over and over again that Jesus was her good shepherd, her vindicator, and that she belonged to Him. I told her that she was strong and more like Jesus every day. I told her that she didn't deserve what she was going through and that I would give my life to see her rescued. She wept harder as her tender little heart thanked me. I ran my finger along her sweet cheeks, rubbing her tears away. I was thankful that she wasn't weeping alone, though I wished she didn't have to cry at all. I wished she wasn't hurting so badly. I prayed and held her quietly.

"Babe, is there anything else you want to tell me today? I know talking about these things is hard, and Auntie will never make you, but if you want to tell me anything else you can. I love you and nothing you could say can change that," I said humbly. She proceeded to share details about her day, gasping for air because her cries had taken on a new intensity.

"Jesus!" I would scream late into the night. "Jesus, You have to come! You have to! Come! Come now! Jesus, for the sake of this one, come now!"

Jesus met me in moments like this all the time—while I held this child in my arms as she wept day after day and in the night as I cried tears of grief and confusion over this precious girl.

One night after navigating an intensely dangerous situation, in which threats had been made to take her life right in front of my eyes and to take mine next, I lay almost lifeless in my bed. Without words, my spirit groaned for Jesus to come and to make Himself known. And His voice boldly declared, *Her name is Sought After.* I opened my Bible and there it was: "They will be called the Holy People, the Redeemed of the Lord; and you will be called Sought After, the City No Longer Deserted" (Isaiah 62:12).

I listened and read the words on the page repeatedly. I believed Jesus and waited on the Spirit, meditating on this passage. Over and over I whispered under my breath, "You call her Sought After, the City No Longer Deserted. You call her Sought After. You say that no longer is she deserted. You call her Sought After. That's her name. She is defined by who You are—the one who seeks her out. This is who she is. She is chosen. She is set apart. She is anointed because You have named her. You have named her Sought After. Her name is Sought After."

The words, replayed over and over in my head and rolling off my lips repeatedly, were like sweet wine to a mature palette. Every time I glanced down and saw what Jesus had written in His Word, I was overwhelmed by the glory of the God I served. I begged the Spirit to take me deeper in revelation about this and to allow me to see this glorious declaration fulfilled. "Jesus!" I cried, "let me see her precisely named and natured in the glory of who You are! You call her Sought After as a mark of Your pursuit of her. You name her in Your pursuit." Glory shook me as I lay there, intoxicated with wonder. The longer I let myself delight in this passage, the more I understood something: in calling this sweet girl Sought After, Jesus was instilling this precise reality into her nature. He wasn't saying this lightly. He was calling her Sought After as a mark of His character. This would eternally tag her as chosen and set apart and deeply instill in her identity the reality that she could not be deserted. Desertion is impossible for someone named Sought After.

I fell asleep with a deeper understanding of Jesus's pursuit of this child. Despite circumstances that rendered her wounded, forsaken, and betrayed, I knew that she was Sought After. I laid my head to rest, knowing that nothing could strip Mutinta of this name.

"Where is the child? Where is the child? The police are after you! We know you have her and the police are coming! When they find you, you will rot in prison! They will feed you to the rats!"

My phone rang off the hook for the next hour, multiple calls from infuriated people, all saying the same thing—that the police were after me. Through bits and pieces of each call, I collected enough information to understand that Mutinta was missing and that I was tagged as the suspect. The police had issued a call-out warrant for my arrest, and they were looking for me. Though I had nothing to do with Mutinta's disappearance and had not had any contact with her in the last few weeks, I knew this was a serious matter. Though I was wholly uninvolved and innocent, fear surged through my body. Blasts of adrenaline jolted me, and questions whirled through my mind. I experienced flashes of heat so strong that I became nauseated and dizzy. Sure, I was nervous for my safety, but even more important, where on earth was Mutinta?

I asked Jesus, "Where is she? Lord, where is Mutinta?" I ran into my room and threw my head into my pillow, though I was filthy from the day. "Where is she? What is she doing? Where is she, Jesus?" Instantly, I saw flashes of her, battered and abused with a spirit of suicide baiting her. I screamed, "No! In Jesus's name, Satan, get away from her!" With flashes of supernatural sight, I saw Mutinta jumping into harm's way but angels surrounding and protecting her. I screamed in agreement, "Yes, Jesus, command Your angels concerning her! Seal her in protection before her and behind her and on every side! I bind evil! Satan, get out!"

I leapt off of my bed and grabbed the keys to my Mitsubishi. I ran out of the house with tears pouring down my face, and I drove. I would find this child. My eyes scanned the masses of people in the streets, looking for her face. *A child so desperate for rescue, where would she be? Where would Mutinta go?* I kept asking myself. I knew in my heart that she would call me if she could. I felt intense anxiety as I thought about where she might be. Was she dead? Had she been abducted? Was she being abused? Was she being raped? Was she in a ditch? Had she been killed? Would I be next? What had happened? I cringed, knowing with perfect confidence that if Mutinta could have called me, she would have. What was keeping her from calling?

My phone rang again, this time a number I knew.

"Sophie, just tell me. Do you have the girl?"

"No. I promise you. I don't have her. I don't know where she is, and I haven't even talked to her in several weeks. I didn't know she was missing until a few hours ago. I don't have her, I promise!"

"You don't have the child? You really don't have her? You really don't know where she is?"

"No," I said again.

"The police are looking for you, and there is a call out for your arrest. You need to be careful because the police have been told that you have stolen the child. All odds are against you. Take some money with you," he said. "That may be the only way out."

"Thanks," I said and began to cry, knowing I would always be unwilling to feed corruption. "I hope you trust me. I will not sleep until Mutinta is found." I put down my phone and started driving again. I could barely make out the ebony figures on the side of the road as my eyes clouded with tears, but I would know Mutinta if I saw her. I blinked rapidly, trying to clear the tears, but they kept coming. My knuckles were white and my stomach was churning. My grip on the steering wheel remained firm, but I was ready to convulse. "Where is she, Jesus? Where is Mutinta? Where is she? I know she would call me if she could. What is happening to her? Jesus! Jesus! Jesus!" I screamed desperately.

I was in agony. A warrant was out for my arrest, and I'd stand no chance with the police. The girl, whom I had spent years fighting for, had been missing for days. I had no idea what had happened, where she was, or what would happen. She hadn't called me, and I knew she would have if she could. If she was alive, she was seriously broken. And if she had been killed, I would die too.

Evening came and still no Mutinta. My life was excruciating, and I couldn't imagine hers. The unknown, the wondering, the terrors ravaging my mind—all this was unbearable. Hours and hours of searching the streets left me empty handed. I wouldn't accept defeat, but the city was huge. I had no idea where she was. All day I had been searching in ditches, in dumpsters, behind gates and shops, in alleyways and markets, and behind taverns. I drove my car into the places where the drug lords ruled and where children were gang-raped daily and through compounds where plastic-bag tents were the only shelter. I scanned miles and miles of streets and studied the faces and the frames of thousands of people. None of them was my Mutinta. As the darkness intensified, my hope was deferred. I'd never find her in the night.

I made it home and found some of my friends enjoying a meal. I immediately felt resentful toward them, underestimating the compassion they would have if they knew about my day. I made it through the doors and sat apart from them. I somberly kept to myself, and all I wanted to do was scream. Did anyone care? Did anyone know the three-year history that I had with this child? Did anyone understand that if she wasn't found, or if she was found dead, I too would die? The accuser came on strong, and never had I felt more helpless. Who could understand this moment?

My heart raced all night. I found my place on a cheap brown sofa and entered into deep intercession. My heart screamed for Mutinta; my being ached for Sought After. I got out a pen and paper, and for hours I cried,

> This I declare over Mutinta, out of Psalm 141:8–10: But her eyes are fixed on You, Sovereign Lord; in You Mutinta takes refuge—do not give her over to death. Keep Mutinta safe from the traps set by evildoers, from the snares they have laid for her. Let the wicked fall into their own nets while Mutinta passes by in safety.
>
> Jesus, fix her eyes on You. Catch her eyes and let her not break her gaze. I speak in Your name. Jesus, be Mutinta's only place of refuge. Be her only comfort, only provider, and only lover.
>
> Jesus, do not give her over to death. Though the grave wants to swallow her up, protect her, Lord.
>
> Jesus, keep Mutinta safe. Let no traps set by evildoers prevail. Jesus, make the wicked fall, that You might receive the glory of her safe return. Jesus, this I believe. This I declare. This I know is true. Answer me quickly, Lord; my spirit fails (Psalm 143:7).
>
> You are worthy. Even now You go before her. You go beside her. You go behind her. She is within your sight.
>
> I believe. I declare. I speak light. I speak wisdom. I speak protection. You go before her. You go beside her. You go behind her.

I speak courage. I speak strength. I speak love over her. I
speak truth, conquering all lies. All lies be gone.

Mutinta, be brought into the light. Reveal yourself quickly.
Stir my belief, Lord. Stir my belief. Have mercy. Listen to her cries.

You go before her. You go beside her. You go behind her.
Shield her. Yes, shield her.

Jesus, reveal Mutinta's whereabouts. Whisper, "I love you" in
her ears. Come to her relief. Give her life right now. Life!

Hold on to her, Lord. Keep her. Hold on to her.

On an on it went—April 9, April 10, April 11. The tally hit seven
days, though I had known about Mutinta's disappearance for only three.
Seven days since she had gone missing, three days since I had last slept.
"Jesus, where is she? If she could call, I know she would. Why hasn't
she called? Jesus, why hasn't she called?" I screamed amid violent sobs,
gasping for air.

☙

Numbness and fatigue paralyzed me as I drove hopelessly through
the streets. Day four. My eyes glazed over, tirelessly looking for that
small frame I'd recognize a mile away. Exhaustion plagued me, and
any adrenaline that had been pumping through my body was now
depleted. I felt terribly weak, not having slept or eaten in days, and I
knew I couldn't do this much longer.

I had met with several juvenile workers and officers in the victim
support unit the day before, and one of them accompanied me to the
police to testify to my innocence and to sit beside me as I endured
the interrogations. The police didn't believe a word I said, but when I
pulled out a forty-five-page, typed case report that I had kept through
the years, their arguments ceased. After spending hours asking me for
money, they finally gave up and released me, lifting the warrant for my
arrest. Though it was nice to know I wasn't going to be hunted down,

nothing in my spirit lifted. Mutinta was still missing, and I would not rest until she was found.

⚭

My phone rang and it was a number I didn't recognize. I quickly grabbed it and pulled it up to my ear, nearly shouting, "Hello? Who is this?"

"It's me, Mutinta." The tone of her voice revealed that she was clearly in danger. "I am in Eden. You have to come. I am hiding. There is a building this side and I am behind the latrines. Come, Auntie!" Though the line had obviously been severed, I screamed back into the phone, "I'm on my way!"

Again, adrenaline rushed through my body as if someone had burst a pipe and it was gushing water. I pushed harder on the gas pedal than I ever had in my life, only to realize I had no idea where Eden was. I panicked and called all the Zambians I knew.

"Hi, Patricia! Do you know where Eden is?"

"Eden? What is that? No, I don't know."

"Joseph! It's Sophie! Can you tell me where Eden is? I am looking for someone in Eden, and I don't know the place."

"What? Eden? No, I do not know the place," he responded.

I scrolled through my phone, going down the list. "Where is Eden?" I cried.

"Sophie, I am sorry. I do not know the place. Maybe somewhere near Soweto Market, that side." I quickly turned my car around to head in that direction, and then I remembered another friend whom I hadn't called.

"John! It's me, Sophie. Listen, you know that child, the one you've helped me pick up many times? Well, she phoned me and she is not okay. She is by Eden, but I don't know the place, John. I don't know the place!"

"Eden? I know the place. Come find me and we will go that side. I will show you the place. Then at least you can have me with you if there is violence that side."

"John, I can't come and get you! You have to tell me the place, and I will go! There isn't time! She's not okay!"

"Okay, so you are going to go like you are headed to Misisi. You need to go past that side; there will be a road that you turn to go down. You will find that filling station next to the tavern, and then you will see the place called Eden."

"Thanks, John. I will phone you later." I hung up. I didn't remember what he had said, but I headed toward Misisi.

"Jesus!" I screamed. "Take me to Misisi!"

I drove for what seemed like hours, my tires kicking up enough dust to suffocate people walking through the streets. "Jesus, where is Eden? Jesus, left or right? Which way?"

I got back on the phone and called one of my friends. "Mutinta called! She's in Eden! Do you know where that is? My friend John told me it's in the Misisi area. Though I know that area pretty well, I've never heard of Eden."

"No, Soph. But let me call one of our field workers who works in that area and see if she knows."

"Okay," I said. I continued to drive and my phone rang again two minutes later. It was my same friend.

"One of our field workers is on her way there now, Soph. Her name is Sheba. I told her you were coming. She is on the main road near the market. She said she is wearing yellow and you will find her. I told her the car you drive, so she is waiting for you. She will take you and help you find her."

"Oh God, thank you so much." I turned my car around yet again, having missed the turn that I knew I needed to take, and I began to scan the masses of people for anything yellow. Sheba would be looking for me, and though I had never met her, I was sure I'd recognize her when I saw her.

After five more minutes of swerving to dodge potholes and maneuvering my steering wheel to avoid trenches and people, I saw a woman in a bright yellow shirt. I threw my head out the window and screamed, "Sheba!" She quickly turned around and jumped in my car.

"Thank you for your help!" I said. "I'm Sophie. This small girl, she is Mutinta. Her story is tragic. She has now been missing for eight days, but she just phoned me, saying she was in Eden, hiding behind the latrines. Do you know the place?"

"Oh, it must be near the station," Sheba said. "Yes, I know the place. Let's go." We drove in silence as terror flooded my mind, twisting and turning through tiny streets and alleys my car could hardly fit through. I drove over burning trash and dead dogs. My vision was so narrow: Mutinta.

As we neared a corner, I saw a small building with chipped green paint. The word *Eden* was barely readable, and my stomach turned inside out. "Just here," Sheba said. Behind the building I saw two small latrines, and I frantically scanned the area. I jumped out of my car, Sheba remaining inside, and ran through the tall brown grass. The stench of feces hit me, stinging my eyes. I quickly wiped away the tears, knowing I couldn't afford to have my vision blurred. *I might never again enjoy a game of hide and seek*, I thought.

I moved forward until I saw a large pile of trash next to a row of thick bushes behind the latrines. I ran there. I grabbed at the overgrowth, saying, "Mutinta. It's me. I'm here." And as I stretched out my arm to take another handful of thorns, there she was. She reached up and grabbed on to me. I had never seen her in a worse state, and I carried her back to my car. My body started to heave as I felt the deepest part of my soul scream for Jesus to come.

⚭

We didn't speak in those initial moments. Mutinta quickly laid herself prone across the backseat, and as I jumped into the driver's seat my knuckles once more whitened with my grip on the wheel. There was no telling what was going on in the minds of the people standing all around us. I just knew I needed to get Mutinta out of there. Sheba picked up on the intensity of the situation and graciously gave me step-by-step directions to a place where we could safely park and find respite.

Every word she spoke was seasoned in poise and compassion. It was obvious why Jesus had chosen her to help me.

About twenty minutes later we found a place to park, and I climbed into the backseat and wrapped my arms around Mutinta. She was weak and frail and covered in blood, dirt, and urine. Her eyes were empty and lost; a chilling numbness masked her face. In all the times I had seen her, even in the heat of past traumas, she had never looked like this. I held her near to my chest, and since she seemed to be slipping in and out of consciousness, I whispered over and over, "Mutinta you are safe now. It's going to be okay. I've got you. You are safe. Come back to me. You are safe in my arms now." Why had she run and what had happened? My mind raced with questions that I wanted to ask her, but Jesus silenced me and calmed my spirit. I had to be wholly present for her and to make certain she understood that she was safe, at least right now.

We remained parked for about an hour, working hard to bring Mutinta out of her daze so she could feel the warmth of my embrace and know she was safe. After another twenty minutes or so, she began to emerge from her traumatic shock, mumbling that she hadn't eaten anything since before she ran away. Sheba and I decided it was best to find food for her. As I returned to the driver's seat, Mutinta lay back down and Sheba leaned over and whispered, "We should be getting food for her, but then she cannot stay with us anymore. She should be going to the police to turn herself in."

Appalled but trying not to raise my voice, I said, "Sheba, no. I will not leave this child alone with the police. They will make her go back to where she was staying."

"Yes, but they can't make her go alone. At least an officer will go with her."

"They won't, Sheba. I just know it."

"Okay, it's fine. You can drop us at the station. I will remain with her so that they can report this. But you cannot come. If they find that you are with the child, then they will accuse you again. That can be too dangerous for you and even more dangerous for her."

I knew I couldn't do anything more at that point. Despite my confidence in Sheba, who regularly dealt with cases of abused children, my heart sank as I quietly agreed.

After a few bites of food Mutinta began to open up. I hadn't expected her to share so soon, but I knew she found much safety in confiding. For that, I was thankful. Mutinta recounted the horrific situation that had caused her to run and how she had concluded it was time for her to die. She confided about how worthless she felt and how the only things that she could think of to do were to start using drugs and jumping out in front of cars. "But Auntie, every time I did, every time I jumped just when a car was going to pass, something stopped it."

Tears poured down my face in a combination of deep grief and great gratitude. Jesus had heard my cries. "One of the street boys pulled me right before I was going to get bashed by one of the cars, and he saved my life," Mutinta said. "Then he told me that God didn't want me to die."

Mutinta continued sharing, and Sheba and I listened intently. Sheba spoke about practical steps for moving forward, which sent Mutinta back into a daze. It was too much.

"Mutinta, I love you," I said. "You are so brave and so strong. I'm so thankful you called me, and I'm so thankful you are still alive. I love you, babe. I will see you soon."

Sheba put her arm around Mutinta, who was hardly able to stand, and said, "Don't worry, Sophie. It's all going to be okay." With that, they got out of the car and began walking to the station.

A few hours later Sheba called me and said, "The police have sent Mutinta back. They refused to let me go with her. They told Mutinta not to tell anyone she was at the police but just to act as if she was lost and she just found her way back. They wrote a report, and they have made a program with the social workers. Sophie, I am sorry. There was nothing I could do."

My heart dropped. I didn't care that the police had written a report or that they had promised a follow-up program. They had just sent a severely abused child back into an incredibly dangerous situation where no one would ever believe the lie that she had been lost. One way or another, Mutinta would be forced to tell the truth.

And what would happen then, only God could know.

A Few Long Days Later

I cautiously entered the small office, and sat down on a felt-like cushion atop a wooden chair. No one was visible, though I could hear voices behind three doors discussing matters unknown to me. A few moments later, a woman whose face I knew very well opened the door and motioned for me to come in. Quietly, I stood up and proceeded into her office.

"Sophie, thank you for coming," she said before three others present as witnesses. "We understand that you have been heavily involved in this child's case now for three years. We have been informed about the child, and we are finding it is a terrible situation. If you can please share your history with the child, you can be of help."

"Yes, I can," I said confidently. For years I had been longing for the moment when I could be a voice for this child who had no voice, and finally I sat before people who had the authority to do something. I told them everything. I read them pages from the report that I had kept over the years. At one point I had two of them in tears, but I didn't let up. For nearly an hour, I shared. I was out of breath and my body was tense, but I was unwilling to stop. For years I had been waiting for authorities to intervene, but every time Mutinta's rescue neared, it never happened.

This time was different. I had the floor and all the proof. Jesus was going to rescue this child. A new home and a new family had been found for her, and the reality of her redemption from years of suffering was coming to pass. Mutinta's rescue was finally happening.

"You can rest tonight," the woman promised me as she excused me from the meeting. "We will go that side, and we will get her. She cannot be there, but we will call for the police to go with us. There will be violence that side, so we will go with them. You can rest. She will be safe now, and you can know you have done a good job. We will go that side tomorrow." Though I couldn't rest until it happened, I knew this was Jesus's good and perfect will. Nothing would stop Him.

The next day came and my spirit was rejoicing. I was still nervous, waiting for the moment when I would receive a phone call confirming that Mutinta was rescued. Doubt came in waves, but I fought it with the words a friend had said to me that morning. "Sophie, nothing anyone says can alter what Jesus has set apart for her. Redemption is here." These words solidified in me as absolute and ultimate truth, and I clung to them. Two o'clock, no phone call. Three o'clock, no phone call. Four o'clock, nothing. At four thirteen I decided to make a call.

"Hello. This is Sophie. Have you managed to get Mutinta?" I asked, my heart now pierced with doubt.

"Sophie, we got the child. We went with the police, got her from that side, and brought her here. She looks very ill and she is very disturbed, but she is saying that you are lying and that she is fine. She told us that she wanted to go back and that she didn't want to talk to you again. So we sent the child back. And she will remain that side. We have removed her case."

The phone dropped from my hand and I collapsed on the floor. I've yet to hear a scream that could match mine at that moment.

∞

Mutinta's story remains unbearable to me. It is still an open wound. Any mention of her name sends fire through my veins, and I ache. My history with this child ended with my greatest betrayal, my greatest horror, and my greatest letdown in faith. This remains an unfinished battle, and her earthly rescue has yet to come. I have no idea where she is, what she is doing, or if she is okay.

I am haunted by the words of my friend that day. Those words were true, but Mutinta's rescue didn't happen. I know Jesus set apart a safe place for her, and nothing anyone said could have altered that, and yet her own words kept her from rescue. She told the authorities I was a liar. She told them my word wasn't true. She told them that I made it all up and that she was fine. The one person in her life whom she knew to be safe, whom she counted on to rescue her when she called, and whom she knew loved her purely, was the one she accused. "Sophie is lying."

I cringe as I imagine Mutinta saying those words in a broken voice with crippling fear and brutal shame. In effect, she was saying, "The one who has shown me more love than anyone on earth, the one I can count on to be faithful to me, the one sent to Zambia for my rescue—I can't count her word to be true." And then I realize these same words are an accurate reflection of my spirit's posture toward Jesus so much of the time. *Jesus, I know You are the one who loves me the most, the one most faithful to me, the one sent, and the one who died for my rescue, but still I can't count Your word to be true.*

This story will always be about a child named Sought After, and I never want any of this to be about me. That day, she named me a liar and walked back into the hands of her abusers, but this had nothing to do with me. She didn't offend me. She couldn't if she tried. She didn't choose to betray me, nor will I ever feel sorry for myself. She made it so far and was so brave, and I ache at the thought of the sadistic threats that must have caused her to deny the one person she knew loved her. I despise the evil that had such a pressing hold on her, and my heart blisters at the thought of her strenuous attempts to find freedom, which always failed. Then I wonder, *What if this is the way Jesus feels about me?*

I've often wondered how Mutinta clung to hope all those years. I sometimes feel an incredible pride in her as I consider how she believed. She taught me so much.

I am still wounded, still hung up on Mutinta's story. I can't coax myself into justifying it with false, comforting theology. I can't make sense of it. I can't handle my confusion. I can't handle the letdown in faith or the tension between what I knew to be Jesus's will and what happened. I can't reconcile the absolute truth that my friend spoke to me with the fact that her words didn't come true. I can't understand why Jesus named Mutinta Sought After, and then when He sought her out and made a way, she wasn't found. She wasn't redeemed in an earthly sense. I cannot understand that. This is a broken place in my faith, an epicenter of doubt, and it's confusing and hurtful. But I have found something: engaging here, with Jesus.

I look at Him and say, "Jesus, what if I, in my confusion and crippled faith, give myself to seeking You out? What if I choose not to allow myself to be okay with this? What if I give myself to forever engaging with You in this mess, not shying away or pacifying myself? What if I ask You to help me learn how to navigate this journey of unanswered prayer without accusing You and without taking it on myself? What if I rest in Your victory that without mistake, has identified Mutinta as Sought After- and forever she will be. And what if I consider that in every broken and crooked turn in my history with Mutinta You spoke something so clear: You named her Sought After, and she was found in Eden.

"Could there be a more precious promise—eternal, untouchable, forever true?

"You named her Sought After, and I believed You. She became Sought After, and she was found in Eden—the place of perfect communion with You, Lord. Eden is the place of fellowship, friendship, and belonging, the garden we so long for. Eden, the place where we are fully known, unashamed, and wholly loved by You.

"Those Sought After will be found in Eden. This is truth."

∽

What I know so intimately from when Mutinta was missing is that I wasn't able rest until I found her. And somehow, I knew that unrest was precisely given as a gift to me to see Jesus magnified. He will have no rest until she is found eternally. In the heat of this crisis, I encountered the zeal and the fire of His pursuit, and I can testify that there will be no rest until the one Sought After is securely found and eternally redeemed. I wouldn't rest until her body was wrapped in my arms, and that was precisely why He created her. He will not rest until we too, are wrapped in His arms forever.

Jesus, I will launch myself into You, trusting You with all that I cannot understand. I will caste myself into Your character, which is not tainted by circumstances. I will forever throw myself into Your faithfulness, which is bigger than disappointment and devastation.

And I will thank You because just like Mutinta, we are all Sought After and we will be forever found in Eden. The spirit and the bride say, "Come!"

CHAPTER 12

AFRICAN FREEDOM DAY

March 2012

At ninety-six pounds and two weeks over term, there she stood. "We have to induce," the doctor said. We knew that was coming, considering Elizabeth's high-risk pregnancy. "Though it is a concern to induce because your body is too thin and the labor will be very difficult, we must."

We sat down in the waiting room for a few minutes as we waited for a nurse. Elizabeth was somber and I could tell she was scared. I was nervous, swaying back and forth between faith and fear. Images flooded my mind, and I fought to gain control. *What if Elizabeth doesn't make it? What if the baby dies?*

Though I looked calm, a war was going on within me. The Enemy desperately wanted to take up residence in the sacred space of my soul, causing me fear and doubt. But Jesus, in His jealousy, graced me with the strength to take every thought captive. I felt His invitation to trust Him and to declare in faith that Elizabeth and her baby would live. His name was much bigger than the concern over this birth, and His love was stronger than the dangerous labor ahead. His promise of life for Elizabeth and her baby was more real than the fear of death.

"Elizabeth," the nurse said. We quietly stood and followed her. I signed papers and paid for Elizabeth's admission into the ward, and we proceeded to the room. In less than five minutes, they induced Elizabeth, and the waiting began. As the nurse left the room she said, "It is going to be a long time before the baby comes. Go to sleep and pray."

∞

I met Elizabeth one day back in 2009 as I was working on an orphan sponsorship initiative. She was the oldest orphan receiving care through this program, and though I didn't know her age, I had overheard someone saying she was more than twenty years old. I would never have believed this had her circumstances not been explained to me. I would have guessed she was a preteen.

I got to know Elizabeth a little bit more in 2010 through a weekly Bible study, but it wasn't until 2011 when our relationship became a beautiful sisterhood. Our time together increased significantly as she spent several afternoons in my home, doing homework and learning basic computer skills to prepare herself for a teaching position she had been offered. It was an absolute delight to have her around so much, and we enjoyed our orange-Fanta-and-grilled-cheese-sandwich dates in my tiny kitchen. Through my probing, she slowly began talking about her past, bravely revealing herself and trusting me with some of her deepest hurts.

I spent a lot of time listening to Elizabeth and praying for her in secret. The story she told on the day I met her had left a mark on me, and the more she shared, the more invested I became in her. The trauma of her childhood was layered and complex, and it was obvious she had yet to truly grieve. No one had ever given her permission.

Despite her wounds, which were deeper than I could imagine, when I looked at Elizabeth I could see a crown of beauty on her head. Though the odds had been against her all of her life, I believed she would find a breakthrough and healing in Jesus and step into His great victory for her.

A complicated unplanned pregnancy was probably the last thing I would have expected for her. Though initially I was devastated and surprised by the news, the trajectory of my hope for Elizabeth shifted. Amid all of the uncertainties and change, hope was still sure: Jesus would be with us, though there was no telling what lay ahead.

⚭

The morning came and her dilation was slow. Around 3:00 a.m. Elizabeth began feeling the first signs of labor, with the agonizing pain starting around 10:00 a.m. "Elizabeth babe, you have to eat something." I knew that with the amount of pain she was suffering the last thing she would want to do was eat, but the doctor had commissioned me minutes before to make the pitch, saying, "Make sure the girl eats. If she doesn't, she won't deliver."

"Elizabeth, here babe, you need to eat." I used my fingers to place small bites of boiled potatoes in her mouth, hoping a few carbohydrates would give her a little more strength. She groaned in pain and clung to the metal frame of the bed, her teeth grinding intensely. "Help, Jesus! Lord, have mercy on me!" she kept yelling.

"God is here, Elizabeth. Jesus has you. He knows your pain. He is here. God is with us. God is with us right now." I felt the Lord press a name for His precious Son on me—Emmanuel, the promise of "God with us." I said that the living promise of God was with us.

"Elizabeth, if it is a boy, how about Emmanuel?" I whispered.

⚭

Labor continued for another six hours before the time finally came for Elizabeth to move to the delivery room. I stepped outside for a few moments and then returned and sat down, only to find that a healthy baby had just entered the world with a strong and glorious cry.

"The baby is a boy," the doctor said.

"Elizabeth!" I whispered as I held her hand. "It's a boy! You have a healthy baby boy! Look at him, Elizabeth! He is beautiful."

"Emmanuel," she said quietly. Tears fell down my face as I watched the nurse wrap baby Emmanuel in a blanket, and I turned back to Elizabeth to see her face as the nurse brought the baby near. Elizabeth's eyes were beginning to roll back in her head. Within seconds, her body began convulsing violently. The nurse yelled for a doctor and placed Emmanuel in my arms. "Go back to the ward," she yelled.

"Wait! No!"

"Now!" she demanded. "Take the baby. The girl is not okay." Unable to argue, I turned to walk out. I looked down at Emmanuel in my arms, just moments out of the womb, and I looked at his mother, now foaming at the mouth and seizing uncontrollably. I felt like someone had just dropped a massive pile of bricks on my chest, making it impossible for air to reach my lungs.

I paced up and down the hallways with Emmanuel in my arms, waiting for any word on Elizabeth. I stared at Emmanuel's face, vowing to him, "I'll never leave you, Emmanuel." I didn't dare say it out loud, for that would uncover my fear and doubt, but I wondered, *What if she dies? Oh, Elizabeth, Jesus! She can't die! No! No!*

Another doctor entered Elizabeth's room, and I tried to see what was going on. I couldn't make out what the doctors were saying. I couldn't bear the agonizing doubt that seemed to be overtaking me, so I returned to Elizabeth's empty room in the ward and sat down. With Emmanuel in my arms, swaddled in a white blanket, I closed my eyes and wept. I couldn't accept death for Elizabeth, but this horrific possibility had gripped my heart. I was terrified but also fierce in my love for this baby. I'd never let go of him if Elizabeth didn't live. And even if she did live, which I begged Jesus she would, I'd still love this child as my own.

Three hours later, Elizabeth was brought back down to the ward. She had lost an incredibly dangerous amount of blood, and she was too weak to keep her eyes open, but she was alive, and she would make it. Though I was still shaken and trembling in my spirit, I began to worship like I had never done before. Where my faith had failed, still

God's faithfulness had prevailed. He had set apart life for Elizabeth and Emmanuel. He had performed miracles and graced me to be a witness. And now His glory would go forth in Elizabeth's testimony and in Emmanuel's miraculous life.

The destiny of this child was wrapped up in his name.

His life would testify to the enduring truth that God is with us.

∞

Following Emmanuel's birth, Elizabeth and I stood in awe over the goodness of Jesus. We laughed and prayed, adoring sweet Emmanuel and looking in wonder at his precious little hands. His big, beautiful eyes were strong, and as I gazed into them I knew he would grow into a God-fearing man. I believed Jesus would in time bring Elizabeth a husband who would love Emmanuel, tenderly fathering him and training him up into godly manhood. When I held him, I could feel the promise over his life, the declaration that his life proclaimed: God with us.

One afternoon when Emmanuel was a day or two over two months old, I went to visit and bring food to Elizabeth. I was going to be out of Lusaka for a few days, so I wanted to make sure she had everything they would need for a while. I surprised her with a week's worth of groceries and some soap and lotion, which she was very excited about. I spent a couple of hours in her one-room home, seated on her mattress on the floor while I held Emmanuel. His big eyes were tired, and ever so sweetly he drifted off into sleep. Oh, to hold Emmanuel in my arms.

"Sophie, I think Emmanuel is sick," Elizabeth she said after about an hour. "I took him to the clinic yesterday, and they gave me medicine for him. But maybe before you go you can leave some money so I can take him to the clinic again tomorrow."

I was slightly surprised since I hadn't noticed any symptoms of illness in Emmanuel. "What did they say at the clinic yesterday?"

"They just said he has a flu. They gave him an injection of medicine."

"Okay, well yes, here," I said as I handed her a bit of money. "If he isn't doing better in the morning, take him to the clinic. Right now he seems okay to me. He's sleeping well and he doesn't have a fever. Has he been sucking well?"

"Not so much," she said.

"Okay, after he wakes up try to feed him again. If he isn't sucking well by this evening, you need to take him to the clinic tonight."

"Okay," she said quietly.

We spent some more time talking, and then we prayed over Emmanuel before I left.

"Elizabeth, call me if you need anything. If Emmanuel isn't getting better, call me right away. Okay? If you call, I will come in an instant. Otherwise, I'll be back in five days."

She walked me out to my car and we exchanged good-byes.

Three days later my phone rang. It was Elizabeth calling.

"Hi, Elizabeth!" I said. "Is Emmanuel okay?"

"No, he's not okay, Sophie. He is very sick."

"What is happening? What did they say at the clinic? What is wrong with him?"

"They haven't said anything, but we have just reached the hospital."

"You are at the hospital?" I said, my voice rising.

"Yes," she replied. "The doctor at the clinic referred Emmanuel to hospital because he is very sick."

"Okay, Elizabeth, I will pack up and come back to Lusaka. Is anyone with you?" I asked.

"Auntie Violet is coming now."

"Okay, good. Elizabeth, when the doctor comes to see Emmanuel please ask what is wrong with him. Have the doctor explain this to you, okay? And I will call you back in a little bit."

"Okay," she said quietly. About half an hour later I tried calling her back, but her phone was off. I tried reaching Violet, who supposedly was on her way to the hospital. On her third attempt she finally answered. "Sophie, the baby is not okay. He is very sick."

Her voice was somber, completely uncharacteristic of her. I began to panic. Though neither of them had said it, I knew Emmanuel was in critical condition. I needed to get back to Lusaka quickly, and an eight-hour drive stood in the way.

∞

I parked my vehicle and I walked briskly toward the main hospital entrance. I made my way through the long corridors, trying to reach the children's ward. My eyes began to water due to the violent stench of the mortuary. Weary men and women lined the halls, staring blankly as I walked by. Their faces had an unnerving stillness, and I tried my best to look deep into each set of eyes. I had been here before, and I knew these halls were home to hopelessness and grief. Most who passed through these doors would leave without someone they loved.

I reached the first children's ward and stepped inside. Nearly lifeless children lay strewn across the floor, and clusters of adults surrounded them, all deeply exhausted. I noticed several women weeping loudly over their children and a few men silently crying as they cupped their hands to cover their faces. A chilling numbness hung over the room, with each person seized by desperation.

I scanned the room and spotted Elizabeth in the very back. Her sunken posture hung somberly over a white metal crib shared by Emmanuel and another infant. I carefully made my way to the back, gently stepping over and around each precious child, and wrapped my arms around Elizabeth. I held her in a strong and tender embrace and then turned my head to peer into the crib where Emmanuel lay.

His tiny body was still except for his lungs, which trembled as he labored to breathe. He was turned onto his right side, a large piece of white tape covering his cheek and holding in place an oxygen line. Several layers of clothing were beneath him, everything stripped away except for a light blue shirt that drowned his tiny, feverish frame. Immediately I reached into the cot and gently placed my hands on his body. I leaned in close and whispered in his ear. It wasn't long before I was heaving, begging for mercy and for Jesus to heal Emmanuel.

After probably twenty minutes, I scanned the room for a nurse or a doctor, but I couldn't find one.

"I'll be right back," I said to Elizabeth. "I'm going to go find a doctor." Again, I carefully made my way back through the room and then down the hallway. I noticed a small office on the right that had a counter and several files, but no one was there. I continued pacing through the hallways, desperate to find a doctor, and finally after about five minutes, a nurse turned a corner and walked my way.

"Excuse me," I said. "Can you please help? I'm looking for a doctor who is working in the children's ward."

"It's just me," she said quietly.

"Oh great. Thank you, Doctor," I said politely.

"No. I'm not the doctor. It's just me here. I'm the nurse. It's a holiday, so there is no other doctor on shift for the night. It's just me. Tomorrow in the morning a doctor will be coming."

"I don't understand." I said, hesitating. "There are at least forty-five children in the ward where my friend and her baby are. There is no doctor for any of those children?"

"No, it's just me, the nurse. And in the three wards, there are ninety-six children total. I have ninety-six patients tonight. No one else is on the schedule for the night."

Horrified and dumbfounded, I looked at her. "What holiday is it?" I asked.

"African Freedom Day," she replied. "These children are all very sick. Most of them will die just like this. They are too far gone. But some of them can make it. I just have to choose."

"What do you mean, choose?" I said, an ever-increasing nausea plaguing me.

"Okay, let me say it like this. If I give medicine and care to one who is going to die anyway, then another will also die. But if I can choose the one who can live, then maybe I can save one. Will you help me?"

It was the most impossible question I had ever been asked. Far from any sort of medical expertise and doused in wild fear, I quietly agreed.

"I will." The depths of my being cried out to Jesus like never before.

In the dark evening hours of African Freedom Day, there I stood along with ninety-six children and one nurse. Oh, Jesus, come.

∽

The nurse escorted me back into the room that I had passed earlier, where all the children's files were kept. As she pulled a few files, I told her about Emmanuel and how he was the reason I was there. I told her that Elizabeth was my dear sister and that the doctor hadn't even told her what was wrong with her son. She quickly found his file and opened it for me to see. In the bottom corner on the first page, there were a few sloppily written notes. Though I couldn't read every word, Emmanuel was suffering from anemia, rapidly progressing pneumonia, and severe dehydration.

The nurse grabbed Emmanuel's file and put a stack of others on top. "First, we will start with these. I will just do an assessment on each of them and start getting them hooked up on IVs. You can go be with Emmanuel, and when I get to that side, then you can help me."

I found Elizabeth seated in a plastic chair with her head resting in her folded hands. She was quiet and didn't see me, but I stood beside Emmanuel and laid my hands on him. I cupped his tiny head and again began to pray, speaking life over him. His emaciated body struggled for every breath—he was fighting for his life.

Standing next to me, a man I hadn't noticed before leaned over the other side of the cot where the other baby was lying. This man's son was much bigger than Emmanuel but still not more than ten pounds. He wiped a cloth over his son's unresponsive body, trying to cool him down and to get his fever to break. I placed my arm on his shoulder, and immediately he began convulsing over his child.

"Danny!" he screamed. "Danny, wake up! Wake up. It's Daddy! Wake up, Danny! Wake up! It's me. My boy, it's me, Daddy!" His voice echoed through the room. I gently took the cool cloth from his fallen hand and continued wiping Danny's skin, hoping for any sign of regained consciousness. His body was dramatically bloated and clammy.

Minutes turned into hours, though time felt at a standstill. Thick, hot tears crept down my face as I watched Emmanuel fighting even harder for each breath while beside him Danny lay freakishly still. I scanned the room for the sole nurse and noticed there were still at least two dozen children between her and Emmanuel. She was working so hard, but the job was impossible. Her face wore the tragedy of ninety-six children nearing the grave. She knew this wasn't freedom.

This can't be real, I thought as tears again welled up in my eyes. I made my way over to the nurse, who was placing an IV in an older girl, who couldn't have weighed more than fifty pounds. The nurse looked wearily into my eyes and asked, "You can help me?" Without thinking, I stepped over and carefully lifted the unresponsive girl's arm out from under the blanket. I rolled up her sleeve and the nurse moved closer.

"Thank you," she said quietly as she pierced her skin with the needle.

I watched this nurse as her tender heart became numb. Her eyes slowly glazed over, though she focused intently to do her job well. Hopelessness had worked its way into her depths, and her eyes betrayed the fearful question within her: *How many of these children will be dead before my shift is over?*

"You need to go," the nurse said as she looked up at me. "Visiting hours were over a long time ago, and you can't be here overnight." Confused and without a response to her stern demand, I slowly made my way back to Elizabeth. She was standing over Emmanuel's crib, squeezing and manipulating her breast in hopes of yielding a few drops of milk. I peered in over the railing of the crib and placed my hand along his tiny back. I began weeping and prayed that his little body would make it through the night. Danny's father joined me, and Elizabeth tucked herself under my arm.

Darkness pressed deep into our bones.

Death was near.

As I said good-bye, I clung to hope that Emmanuel would survive the night. I couldn't imagine Elizabeth being alone, watching her baby boy struggle for every breath. Emmanuel's heaves had progressed into desperate gasps for air—it was too much.

The clock reached midnight as Elizabeth pulled out from our embrace. With sobs building in my gut, I whispered, "I'll be back at six. I love you."

I bent over Emmanuel and kissed his tiny cheek.

"I love you, brave boy. I'll see you in a few hours."

With that, I walked out. I made it home and laid myself down, sad and angry that the nurse hadn't let me stay. At 3:07 a.m. my phone rang with news too much to bear.

Emmanuel was gone.

I stood up, washed my swollen and blotchy face, and walked out the door. Later I wrote in my journal,

May 26, 2012

The floor is cold; seated, I rest. I look ahead, and my beautiful Elizabeth lies almost lifeless. Breath fills her lungs, though I know she wishes it wouldn't. Her eyes are shut, but somehow I know she's not sleeping. Shock and pain mark her.

Flies buzz violently as my feet rest outstretched. I don't bother to swat at them. I am ever conscious of life and will do nothing to take it away, not even from a fly.

To my right, women gather outside. Heads wrapped and somber they sit, cooking nshima. I notice their chairs, which hold up and support their bodies. And all I can think of is the IVs and the medicines that did not support Emmanuel's body.

His little lungs gasping for every breath. His body so weak yet fighting. Last night I said good-bye, my eyes filled with doubt but my spirit with belief that the morning would reveal improvement.

I cannot understand how two months and six days ago, I held my 2.8-kg Emmanuel, tiny but filled with life. I cannot put a price on the first breaths that he took in my arms. His nose, cute as ever, brought tears to my eyes. My miraculous God was evident.

Then today I held my 3.0-kg Emmanuel, tiny, withered, and lifeless. I stood near last night as he approached his final breaths, speaking life over him, trying so hard to believe. His nose, still precious, brought tears to my eyes. My humanity is evident along with the vapor that this life truly is.

I cannot understand. Nothing is clear. Nothing makes sense. I feel pain, yet I know Jesus is still good.

One nurse for ninety-six children. Dying children. The rest of the doctors and nurses on holiday, African Freedom Day. Nothing about this situation resonates with freedom.

Not just my Emmanuel, two months old. Also my new friend Danny, five months old.

One bed. Two little boys fighting for their lives.

2:30 a.m. Emmanuel takes his last breath.

3:00 a.m. Danny does too.

Last night I wept with Danny's father. We prayed over Danny, ushering him in to the presence of Jesus. We wiped cool cloths over his body, trying to break his fever. He was unresponsive. Little did I know that this morning his body would be stacked among the others—maybe even thrown in. The morgue isn't suitable even for dogs, let alone for precious children.

This morning we dressed Emmanuel in a sweet little outfit, the one I bought for him when he was born. A little blue turtleneck with three cars on the front. Blue sweat pants with turquoise stripes down the sides. Thick socks—baby blue In color—and his sweet little hat. His emaciated body was drowned in them. Those clothes, purchased to celebrate life, now cover him in his earthly death.

The burial is happening now. Elizabeth is not there and neither am I. The father, who met Emmanuel only yesterday, said that it was their custom to bury the same day and that the mother isn't allowed to come. I cannot understand this, but I won't argue. I know Elizabeth cannot watch her baby boy being lowered sloppily into the ground. Not today. Not ever.

Elizabeth falls into my arms, screaming, "My baby is gone! Sophie, my Emmanuel, he's gone!" Her body shakes unceasingly. Tears flood my eyes, and all I know to do is to hold on tight. I weep despite my every attempt to remain composed.

The morgue is a sick place. They asked me if I would go in to identify Emmanuel among the shelves stacked full with bodies. Thankfully, someone else did. I'm not sure I could have done it.

His casket is as small as a shoebox. Tiny and wooden, it's all I can think of. And Danny's casket is only a bit bigger. I wonder where his burial is taking place. Somehow I wish they could be buried side by side.

My teeth aren't brushed. My hair is not washed. My body stinks, and my eyes burn like fire. My lips are chapped and cracking, and I can't even remember what it feels like to have an appetite. Exhaustion plagues me and I am so sad.

Two months and six days.

I know it wasn't Jesus's will that Emmanuel died, nor was it His will for Danny to die. His will is not to leave families mourning—ever. But Jesus is sovereign and heaven is real. That is the only hope here.

So Jesus, though I don't understand, I confess my humanity and I throw off all that hinders. I proclaim that I know You are sovereign, and I know that heaven is real. And I know that Emmanuel and Danny are with You today.

Oh, the truck just got here from the burial. The first things carelessly thrown out of the back are three shovels used to dig Emmanuel's grave. The dirt, fresh and dark, sticks to the metal heads of the shovels, and I just close my eyes.

PART 4

BY HIS STRIPES

"Surely he took up our pain and bore our suffering, yet we considered him punished by God, stricken by him, and afflicted. But he was pierced for our transgressions, he was crushed for our iniquities, the punishment that brought us peace was on him, and by his wounds we are healed."

—Isaiah 53:4–5

13
CHAPTER

SONGS OF DELIVERANCE

The cords of death entangled me; the torrents of destruction overwhelmed me. The cords of the grave coiled around me; the snares of death confronted me. In my distress I called to the Lord; I cried to my God for help. From his temple he heard my voice, my cry came before him, into his ears. The earth trembled and quaked, and the foundations of the mountains shook; they trembled because he was angry ... He reached down from on high and took hold of me; he drew me out of deep waters. He rescued me from my powerful enemy, from my foes, who were too strong for me. They confronted me in the day of my disaster, but the Lord was my support. He brought me out into a spacious place; he rescued me because he delighted in me.

—Psalm 18:4–7, 16–19

The thick brown grasses of June swayed in the cool morning breeze as I made my way up the mountain. Tangled bunches of my long

113

blond hair whipped my face, eventually finding their resting place in the corner of my mouth. Dense dust settled between my teeth like sandpaper, and my abdomen tensed with hunger pangs. I had wept through the night, but the morning had come with promise.

Tears trickled down my face as the brisk air enveloped my weary eyes. My quadriceps burned deeply, almost as if they had been set ablaze by the climb, and my gaze was fixed optimistically on the nearing plateau. It was a Thursday, the second-to-last day of a rural orphan outreach I was on, and I could feel Jesus near me. I knew it wouldn't be long before many feet, big and small, would make their way up this mountain. I had heard Jesus's voice, and based on the warfare I had endured in the night, I knew He wanted to release a beautiful and unprecedented freedom. I was certain that Jesus was going to shake up the dust, destroy strongholds, deliver the demon-possessed, and unleash a wild and untouchable freedom. And freedom that comes from Jesus's hand is always stunning.

I reached the plateau and sat down on the hard, dry ground. I pulled out a long, thin rag and tied up my hair, imagining the yanking my scalp would have to endure at dusk. I focused on catching my breath and steadying my posture and my spirit before the Lord.

Images of the children who I knew would be coming flooded my mind, and I saw deep strongholds called out by a tender God. I envisioned an army of angels coming to set a seal over the mountain, and I believed that Jesus would reach down from on high to touch us.

Soon small ebony frames made their way up the hill. My eyes had once been weary, but now they felt different. A subtle and precious confidence settled into my depths as I watched these broken ones draw near.

Today had already been paid for.

She hadn't said but two words the entire week. I had met her four days earlier, but not once had she cracked a smile or allowed herself to relax. She wore a jean skirt and mismatched shoes with layered white socks beneath. Her thirteen-year-old eyes looked aged and weary, and her sunken posture reflected a history I couldn't imagine. As I looked at her face, uniquely striking and round, the artist in me saw canvas for an infectious smile.

But she was on lockdown.

Beauty is often locked behind bars.

Each day as I went out to share the Word, this girl would come to hear but then get up and walk away. She would wander for a while, apparently aimless, and return to sit back down. Any mention of Jesus caused her to leave again. She wouldn't sing. She wouldn't play games. She wouldn't let me give her a hug and wouldn't even take a cup of cold water from my hands. Pain marked her.

The nights were long on this visit to rural Zambia. Every dark hour, as I rested within the unfinished mudded walls of what passed for a house, my spirit landed on her face. Her plight and her bondage became the agonizing groan of my spirit, and I wondered if she was possessed by demons. I wasn't certain, but if she was, I knew it wasn't her fault. I didn't want to make any assumptions, so I continued to pray and to ask for discernment. I thrashed in my bed with searing pains in my back, and a horrifying chill swept through the room. Jesus's heart was obviously set on clothing her in freedom, but the garments He paid for don't always show up on our runways.

◌◌

I spotted her as she made her way up the hill, mixed in with about a dozen other children. The others were chattering, a few of them were holding hands, and two were singing. As they came into clearer view, I saw her staring back at me with an empty gaze. I could tell that a seal had been placed on her in the spiritual realm, and images flooded my mind. Though I didn't know any details of her story, I did know that she had repeatedly been declared unclean and that even she believed it. Though Zambia has no official caste system, it was obvious that the label had landed this precious girl at the bottom.

I watched her as she continued up behind the other children. Her stride was deeply hesitant; she was fighting obvious opposition. Her posture was strained and exhausted, and the tightness of her brow revealed an intense battle. I kept my eye on her as the other children neared, and as each of them cheerfully reached the plateau and found little rocks to sit on, I took a few steps in Espina's direction. She immediately retreated backward and began shouting, almost barking. In that moment, I became certain that she was under a demonic influence, and I immediately felt a generous boldness to share the gospel completely unhindered.

I began to share the gospel, from Genesis to Revelation. It was as if I could see the soil of each heart, and with every heart that had good soil, more boldness came over me. It soon became obvious that the Spirit wanted to completely take over, and so I stopped.

"I'm going to stop teaching and we are going to place ourselves at the footstool of heaven," I told the children.

At that moment, fourteen hearts were set ablaze in hunger. Espina, who had made her uncharacteristic entrance just moments before, calmly sat down right beside me and looked straight into my eyes.

Almost immediately her eyes darted away and her body convulsed. I prayed and waves of strong and passionate voices followed. Within moments the children had their faces in the dirt; some were weeping, some were yelling, and some were even laughing. I prayed in the Spirit as I waited patiently to hear the next move from the Lord. To my knowledge, none of these children had ever opened their hearts to the gospel, and this may have been the first time some of them had encountered Jesus.

I felt the Spirit nudge me and I laid hands and prayed for these children. It was a clear opportunity to administer the presence of the Holy Spirit, but I was fully aware that these moments had nothing to do with me and everything to do with Jesus's pursuit of these children and with binding up their brokenness.

Espina was now seated with intense anger across her face. I calmly approached her and gently placed my right hand on her head. She pulled away, falling down in the dirt, and immediately I could tell that the little girl inside of her was held captive by darkness. I got down in the dirt beside her and proclaimed freedom over her. I could hear her calling out, "Jesus! Jesus!" and then suddenly she would stop. I made no retreat and simply continued to declare freedom in Jesus's name.

Espina thrashed around on the ground for quite a while, sometimes extending her hands up to the sky but kicking up a dust storm. She screamed as if her entire body was chained, and I stood in agreement with Jesus as He ordered the demons to let go. An image flashed in my mind. I saw us climbing up the side of a mountain, and we were almost at the top. I glimpsed the scenery, and it was beautiful. There was rest in this place. Then the Lord brought to light the last moment before reaching the top and showed me it was the place of the greatest toil and the greatest agony.

The climax of the breakthrough things of God is always the hardest stage. But once it is conquered, freedom rushes in like a raging river.

"Jesus! Jesus! Jesus!" Espina screamed as she reached toward the heavens. "Jesus, save me! You save me! Jesus!"

Over and over the name Jesus flew from her lips as her hands pressed harder toward the heavens. Tears made the dust turn to mud on her face. For more than an hour she screamed, "Jesus! Jesus! Jesus!" All of the children wrapped themselves tightly in my arms. We contended for fire to purge all the lies that for so long had taken root, and we made room for Jesus to minister to us all. As Espina brought herself to her knees, I gently helped her out of the dirt. I got her cleaned up while one of the children fetched her a small jar of water.

I brought all the children into a tight circle, and we sat on the top of this mountain. It was a much smaller mountain than the one Jesus had showed me, but nonetheless we were at the top. Jesus had touched us in such a way that there was no need to tie up loose ends or to discuss with the children what had been happening. They all knew. They had all encountered Jesus and were all new creations—forever saved and made whole in His presence and eternally changed. Their eyes, every single set, looked different. These children, who had come broken and hopeless, were now alive. One encounter with Jesus changed everything. They were wildly free—free to love and to be loved.

Even Espina.

I rose the next morning with swollen eyes and a grateful heart. I had sobbed through much of the night, immensely thankful for what Jesus had done. My soul was singing songs of praise, and my mind was replaying the huge deliverance manifested in the lives of many children, including sweet Espina. I envisioned what she would look like the next time I saw her. I prayed that I'd have a chance before leaving the bush. I couldn't imagine the testimony that would come from her lips, though I knew it would be preciously beautiful—so telling of sweet Jesus.

I placed my feet on the cold cement floor and rose from the mattress. I quickly changed my clothes, strategically layering to accommodate the brisk morning that would give way to the oppressive noonday Zambian sun. My skirt wisped the ground as I walked toward a small brazier, already lit with hot coals. The morning was dark and quiet, and I was eager for the day ahead.

I made my way down the long dirt path toward the mountain where I had been meeting with the children. As I neared, the incline steepened and I remembered the burning in my quadriceps. The day before, I had contended for fire, but I now took each step rejoicing because the Holy Spirit had descended. I was excited to see the children, whose little voices were music to my ears. As I hiked, I declared to God, "You are my hiding place; you will protect me from trouble and surround me with songs of deliverance" (Psalm 32:7).

As I approached the plateau I heard their voices. I had assumed they would all return, but I wasn't expecting them to be early. To my surprise, as my eyes became level with the ground, I saw every child already seated and waiting for me. And right in front of me, Espina stood with a radiant smile. She jumped into my arms, and with tears streaming down our faces. We sang a song of thankfulness.

Jesus changes lives.

> "My name is Espina. I am an orphan, no mum and no dad. When my parents died, the witch doctor told me I was cursed. They told me I was the one who killed mum and dad. I believed them from that time. The demons would come in the night and

tell me that they could make me clean from the curse, but I had to invite them into me. So I did. I never felt clean, but they always whispered that I was a good girl and that soon I would be free from the curse. That was a long time ago.

But then I came here. I came and I would hear someone say 'Jesus' and my body would pain, and it hurt me very much. My demons would tell me to run away, so I did. But as I was hearing the words and hearing about Jesus, my heart was telling me to listen. I couldn't manage, but then it happened. My heart listened and I knew it couldn't be the demons that would make me clean. It had to be Jesus. I don't know what happened, but I just reached up and screamed for Jesus. My body was hurting and I was yelling, but it could only be Jesus who could clean my soul.

It wasn't me who killed my mum. It wasn't me who killed my dad. I am not cursed. When everyone was praying for me it was like the demons had to get out. They went out. Jesus has saved me. Now I feel happy and I know the truth. I am clean and I can smile. And no demons came to me in the night. Jesus has saved me! Now I am free!"

One year later I made it back to that same village. The Spirit had prompted me that morning to forfeit my plans for the day and to jump on a bus and go.

I arrived and got off the bus with no idea how the day would pan out. I contemplated taking a taxi to the compound where some of the children had come from, and I also considered going up to the mountain again. I stood at the side of the road and asked the Lord but heard nothing. I was frustrated, so I began walking. I hadn't brought anything with me, just a little money to get food and water for the day and then a bus ticket back, so I walked and prayed.

As the hours passed I felt aimless and increasingly annoyed. I wanted to be pure in heart, but I felt too tired. I struggled as I talked to Jesus, dragging accusation and pride into the conversation while He remained steady and unchanging. The Rock of Ages is never moved by my frenzy.

In my frustration I decided to turn around and to head into the compound before catching a bus back to Lusaka. As I was turning, someone jumped on my back. My knees buckled and gave way, and I fell to the ground.

"Mama Sophie!" she screamed.

I spit the dust out of my mouth and turned around to see who it was. Espina beamed from ear to ear. I grabbed her, wrapped my arms around her tightly, and began weeping. I couldn't believe my eyes.

"Just wait. I'm coming!" she said as she jimmied her way out of my embrace.

"Wait? Where are you going?"

"I'm coming!" Espina said and kept running. About two hundred yards ahead, she stopped at a little shop that sold vegetables. I saw her reach into her pocket and give the lady inside a small bill. Espina extended her hand and then sprinted back to me.

"Mama! It's for you!"

I put my arms out to embrace her as I watched her run. She was more beautiful than I had ever seen her, and she surely had grown. She looked straight into my eyes and said, "Here! I love you!" I reached out and she dropped the little treasure from her hand into mine.

"It's chewing gum," she said. Sure enough, she had just purchased a tiny pink gumball for me. "Eat it. It's nice."

"Thank you, Espina," I said, looking into her eyes. I placed the little gumball in my mouth and savored every ounce of sweetness. I was absolutely overwhelmed. I couldn't find any words, but what I wanted to say was that no one had ever given me a gift so huge and blessed me so richly. I wanted to look her in the eye and say, "Espina, you have no parents. You have no money except enough to buy a single gumball. And you bought one for me?"

"Yes, Mama! I love you!"

We spent a few minutes together, but then it was time for her to return to her chores. She was in charge of preparing the nshima for her auntie and her cousins that night. As we said our good-byes I looked deep into her eyes and then whispered in her ear, "I love you, Espina. Thank you for the chewing gum. You have blessed me more than I could ever repay you. I love you." I kissed the top of her head, squeezed her tightly, and off she went.

"I love you too, Mama. I'll see you soon!"

Waves of grateful sobs came over me as I made my way to the bus station. When the bus arrived and I climbed up the steps, the driver saw my tears and asked me, "Has there been a funeral?"

"No," I said. "More like a resurrection."

☙

Espina's story of deliverance is beautiful, without a doubt. I am consistently humbled that Jesus saw fit to bring this child into my life, grateful unto eternity. He did this for the sake of her redemption and deliverance but equally (if not more so) for the sake of my redemption.

I flash back to Espina in the dirt, extending her hands to the heavens, screaming in unrelenting pain. I remember the piercing depth of her screams, so telling of the distress in her spirit. Her past and present circumstances were horribly unjust but precious since they produced desperation in her rather than offense.

Espina knew her need.

I can still feel the aches that I had in my body as I contended for her freedom. I remember the glorious soreness I felt in my cheeks after the Spirit had descended on the mountain and all we could do was scream and shout with joy, smiles wide across our faces. I can still taste that sweet pink gumball on the tip of my tongue.

I never want to forget.

And I never want to forget that I need Him.

It is here that Espina's story wraps itself around me. I am left undone, swaddled in the truth that the perfect author of her story is the same one penning mine—the one who created me to need Him.

I want to live every day, pressing my hands toward heaven and screaming for Jesus, just like Espina did. I want to hunger so badly and ache so deeply that I am overtaken by wordless groans. I want to call out Jesus's name as only someone who is completely desperate would, because I know He will come in fullness.

He will surround us with songs of deliverance.

He may even come with a wide smile and a pink gumball in hand.

If only we might know our need.

14
CHAPTER

HEALED IN HIS PRESENCE

Then I thought, "To this I will appeal: the years when the Most High stretched out his right hand. I will remember the deeds of the Lord; yes, I will remember your miracles of long ago. I will consider all your works and meditate on all your mighty deeds." Your ways, God, are holy. What god is as great as our God? You are the God who performs miracles; you display your power among the peoples. With your mighty arm you redeemed your people, the descendants of Jacob and Joseph.

—Psalm 77:10–15

I made my way out of my house and ventured down the tarmac to jump on the first blue-and-white minibus on the three-stage route I needed to take. It was the weekend and I was heading for a small church in the compound where I met many women for weekly prayer gatherings. I was excited to see their faces and to sing loudly with them. (There isn't a more beautiful sound than the singing of Zambian women packed into a small concrete church.) I reached the bus stop and a minibus pulled over and opened its door. The bus was full but I squeezed in the back, shifting my small backpack into my lap as two other passengers piled tightly in around me. Such is life in the Zambian minibus system.

Waves of body odor flooded my nostrils, and I did my best to avoid thinking about it. The hot afternoon air felt like a blow dryer too close to my face, and I started to get nauseous. Soon, my legs began to lose their feeling.

A few minutes into the ride, the man seated beside me, who reeked of alcohol, grabbed me and began forcing himself on me. Though my hands were caught around my bag, I tried to pull away from him. When he finally let go, my head slammed on the glass window beside me. I was startled and I yelled. Within seconds, the commotion on the bus was so great that even people in the front were shouting. As the other passengers forced the man off of the bus, I sat quietly in the back corner, breathing deep. Vaguely numb, I thought, *All in a day's work.*

A few moments later the driver pulled over and I got off of the bus. I thanked the conductor, though I was annoyed about the ride, and I made my way to the next place, where I would take a taxi-share. I stood quietly as the taxi filled, and then I got in for the five-minute ride to the small dirt road in the heart of the compound.

At a dusty intersection, I got out and walked the remainder of the way, about a half-mile. Each week I came eagerly to this gathering because Jesus always moved. But even more important than the major growth that He was producing in all of us individually was the slow and steady work that He was doing, causing us to become a family. It was energizing to spend week after week studying the Bible together while living beside each other. Something so beautiful takes place when you live in authentic community.

In this place I was given a much deeper revelation of what God intended for family. What a privilege it was to partner with Jesus in what He was doing in these people's lives while seeing how they partnered with Him in what He was doing in my life. Every moment we spent together was tenderly purposeful. I always felt Jesus pursuing my heart when I was with these precious women, and I began to understand how much His heart desires that we have community like this.

I made my way into the church through the metal-framed door and was welcomed with shrieking and clapping. Dancing immediately ensued and I felt my face beaming. It was still slightly difficult for me to enter this place, knowing there was still so much circulating in the compounds about me, but my heart found refuge as I felt the presence of Jesus already among us. It was truly sweet. We sang and danced and acted like giddy little girls, twirling together playfully, and naturally from there, we moved into worship. The progression was simple—joy unto joy, glory unto glory. We knew that Jesus had given us all the good in our lives, and oh, did we sing.

In a normal prayer meeting, we would have worshiped for a while and then carried on in prayer and studied the Word together. It was my goal to go deep into the Word with these women and together to walk out the truth. However, on this particular day I felt that the Holy Spirit had a different plan.

As we worshiped, a thickness fell on the room that brought all fifteen of us to our knees and invited us to join the Lord in deep intercession. Within seconds, a sea of tears began to flow, though we were not sad. Jesus, our great intercessor, had come near, and we were joining Him in His great intercession.

A woman named Abigail began to pray out loud. As she prayed, she shouted and praised Jesus, calling forth His goodness and His faithfulness. She boldly shouted the truth about God back to Him, and the rest of us stood in absolute agreement. In accord with Zambian tradition, we prayed simultaneously, and the sound erupting from within the concrete walls of the church was enough to inspire anyone. The presence of the Spirit was intense, and I knew Abigail was anointed to preach the Word to us.

We carried on for a few hours, though we weren't even slightly aware of the time. At one point I looked up and I saw three of my dearest sisters with puddles of tears on the floor beneath them. As I watched the tears fall and hit the concrete, repelled by the fresh cobra wax that must have been applied just the day before, I noticed that the puddles were joining into small streams. Together, the Spirit and the bride say come.

Abigail brought the word, though at first it was difficult for me to listen. Several parts of her body were swollen, and a deep black eye dominated the entire left side of her face. After contemplating whether it would be appropriate to question her, I interrupted and asked, "Abigail? What happened?" She nodded and said, "Yes, I know that I must tell you." Fear gripped me for my precious mama, and my mind raced as she hesitated before speaking again. Quietly and with great courage, she recounted the abuse she had endured just hours before.

She spoke for about ten minutes and then wrapped up by saying, "Now I am coming from the place of being beaten and I am here. My body is paining very much, but there is power in the name of Jesus! Now I will preach the gospel with power for you because when I am weak, then I am strong!"

We all sat in awe of Abigail, but she wasted no time in getting to the word she had prepared for our prayer meeting. All of us were completely humbled by her obedience and her faithfulness while also moved to deep compassion for her. Abigail's diligence and joy, just hours after being beaten, were incredible and ministered hugely to us all. As she gave the devotion, Jesus gave me a vision of the ministry time that would follow Abigail's message. Jesus wanted to physically heal these women, and my hands began to feel the fire of heaven.

Abigail wrapped up, and all of us clapped and began singing and dancing, making lots of noise again for Jesus. It was so beautiful. We returned to prayer and I declared the Lord's plans over the meeting. I quietly moved back and forth in the narrow church, and soon I saw images in the Spirit of the healings that Jesus was going to release. The pain in Abigail's limbs and face would be wiped out—she'd be pain-free before leaving the church. Violet would be healed of ongoing migraines. (I didn't know she was having them.) Another woman would be healed of intense pain in her heels, and she would walk home pain-free. Another woman, whose husband lay ill at home, would return to find him up and cooking for the family. I was filled with great faith, and boldness overwhelmed me. I spoke forth each one of these situations, and as I did, the Spirit of God lifted each infirmity.

I don't remember much more of the meeting from that point, other than the fact that it was glorious. We were caught up in the glory of God, and heaven surely had come near. I still recall the extreme joy that fell over me the moment I realized that it was getting dark outside, indicating we had been in the church for several hours. As we closed, I said, "Next week is testimony week. Just testimonies." And I laughed.

Before long we left the church healed and expecting more healing. Violet was the last one out before we locked up the church, and I could sense there was still an ounce of discouragement in her spirit despite the glory of the day. After locking the door, I took her hand, prayed for her, and then looked into her eyes and said, "Whatever you ask for according to His will, you shall have. By the time you reach home, it will be yours. Go in faith, sweet mama. I'll expect you to be leading next week. Your testimony is huge." And with a big hug, we parted ways.

∞

One week later, there she was, gloriously glowing. Violet stood in the door of the church, waiting for me to arrive, and she sprinted toward me with open arms. "Sophie! Sophie!" she yelled. "I am healed! And even now, more are being healed!"

When all the women arrived, Violet shared her incredible testimony and later recorded it in my journal:

> "For a long time I was sick and I was not feeling well, and people were trying to get me to go to the witch doctor and to receive healing and medicine there. But I didn't. I didn't go there, but I trusted only in the Lord. Last Friday when I went to prayers, Sophie prayed for me. Immediately when Sophie prayed for me, I went home and I was healed. I felt like my headache wanted to come back, but after Sophie prayed, it didn't. I know that prayer. I don't know where it came from, but it's from God. Since I've known Sophie, I have never heard her praying like I heard that day.

She prayed a really powerful prayer. When I went home I slept. It was a good prayer for me, and I slept like a baby. So I was healed!

Then I went to my neighbor and I said, "Maybe I can pray." She had a headache and a backache, and she had a problem with her stomach. On her back she had a lot of water, so when she went to the hospital they said they would have to do a lung puncture.

For six months she was bedridden. When she woke up she would say, "I've got a headache. My leg has sores, and I am not feeling well at the back." So it was like she was bedridden. She wasn't going anywhere. Then I said, "In the Lord there is no need for a lung puncture to remove the water and the pains. So I will pray for you. There will be no lung puncture or other things." When I prayed for her, she got healed! Immediately when I prayed for her, she got healed!

The next morning she went to the hospital, and they said, "No, we won't do the lung puncture. It's okay. We don't see any problem. You are healed!"

I'm really a changed person. It's a miracle, a testimony! There are miracles in God. When you pray for the sick they will be healed. And when you believe, God is going to answer you."

First Violet was healed. Then she prayed for someone else, and that person was healed too!

This testimony still leaves me in absolute awe and gives me fantastic joy. Jesus showed up in such a beautiful way. We wept, partnering with Him in intercession. We heard the word, anointed and fierce. We witnessed bruised faces and swelling disappear. We heard shrieking as heel pain left, and we had a full-on dance party. Most important, we left knowing that God is a God of testimony.

Violet didn't know that day when she came to prayers that she would be healed. (None of the women did.) She didn't know that she would encounter Jesus Himself and that He would lift the pain from her body. She wasn't aware that at the core of His character Jesus is a healer and that this truth was true for her.

Violet also didn't know that power would come upon her when she received His healing and that faith would take such deep root in her. When she reached out to her neighbor she didn't know if this person would be healed. But she did know after being healed herself that Jesus could do it and that He was willing.

Jesus responds to testimonies about His goodness and faithfulness. Our testimonies of Him tug at His heart. When we stand on His promises from days of old, our faith moves His heart to respond to our cries for healing.

He needs no reminders of what He can do. But when we bind ourselves to the truth of His ability, declaring that He has done it before and can do it again, something deep inside of Him is moved.

Jesus is moved by His own goodness.

We are healed in His presence.

He is a God of testimony.

CHAPTER

SHE WILL BE CALLED
A MIGHTY OAK

June 2009

A baby's first cries were heard in a small mudded home in the heart of one of Lusaka's poorest shanty compounds. A twenty-nine-year-old woman lay bare on the dirt floor of her mother's home. Her violent screams had endured through the night, but the Lord's favor saw her through to the morning. With no money to pay for a delivery in a clinic, this woman's mother knelt at her daughter's side and watched her precious granddaughter come into the world. The baby's uncle and grandfather were somewhere near, and both came to see the new baby. Sometime that day the family made a joint decision and named the child. Everyone was thankful that the baby girl seemed healthy despite the mother's severe illness. It was obvious that God had favored her womb.

Around the same time, just on the opposite side of the capital city in another compound, a nineteen-year-old foreign woman lay bare on the cold concrete floor of her tiny home. She too had been weeping and groaning through the night. As with the woman across the city, the Lord's favor carried this woman to morning. Around sunrise she surrendered and committed to the Lord to be obedient to His purposes for her in this foreign nation. She had no money or the means to understand the magnitude of the commitment she had made. Despite her exhaustion, as she picked herself up from the floor she rejoiced and poured out her thankfulness to the Lord. She was grateful that He had spoken richly from the book of Esther about relief and deliverance for the children of Zambia and had favored her willingness and her yes. Despite this young woman's unlikeliness to make any lasting mark on the children in the nation of Zambia, God had favored her and set apart for her a distinct inheritance. God's favor was upon her, and she gave birth to a vision of laying down her life for the orphan.

Though the two women had no idea, a gift so precious was given to each of them in the very same moment of time. Both of them were humbled and on the floor, positioned to receive an explicit mark of honor and favor from the Lord. The God of the universe set in motion a glorious move of His faithfulness, justice, and redemption as His hand brought forth a precious baby girl from the womb of one. In His glory and sovereignty, the womb of another woman's heart was opened, and she made a commitment that would lead her to this same precious baby girl.

∞

The clock neared midnight on December 31, 2009, and I stood before the Lord. As the new year quickly approached, I gave myself to contending for His presence and for the Holy Spirit to come with fire. I was excited and invigorated by the fresh inspiration and natural reminder of the new that comes with the new year. I was energized and inspired to reach deep into the heart of God and to hear from Him about the year to come. My heart was postured in such willingness to hear, and I was full of expectation and was desperate for His voice.

I waited and continued to worship. With about five minutes left before the start of the new year, I said, "Jesus, speak of what You have for me this year. Speak tenderly to me; do not put me to shame. Let me see Your face. Let me hear Your voice. I long for Your voice, beloved." My mind flooded with thoughts about what Jesus might say, distracting me. I quickly grew frustrated, as if my proneness to wander in thought could hush the voice of the Lord if He chose to speak.

The clock struck 12:00 a.m., and with my spirit alert and sober, I began to face the reality of what lay ahead of me. Ever so gently, like cool running waters, I felt in my depths that God was calling me to motherhood.

I stood for a few moments, trying to process what He was doing. I was confused and even offended, wondering why He would speak to me about motherhood at the start of this new year. Ever since I was young I knew I would be a mother someday, but a reminder of that in this season didn't make sense to me. *Maybe He's just putting motherhood on my heart in a hypothetical way,* I thought. *Maybe this is more like being a mama to all the kids I see each day.*

I left it at that. I didn't dig much deeper into what God was impressing on my heart, and quite frankly, I was a bit apathetic about His prompting. It just didn't seem too significant.

∽

Normal life continued in Zambia. Though I was still confused, I asked Jesus to freshly excite me, and I intentionally pursued each child I came across with the heart of a mother. I started to care more deeply about what the Lord had put on my heart, and though it's obvious now that I missed the point, I persisted in asking Jesus to manifest Himself completely in every opportunity I had with a child. The time I was spending in a village about an hour from the city proved to be an incredible opportunity to love many children. I also was spending more time in a crisis orphanage, which always proved intense and heartbreaking, but it was an incredible opportunity to speak life over each precious child.

One night in early February I sat in a chair at home and discussed my day with Jesus. The day had been particularly hard on many levels, and my struggle exposed strong feelings of loneliness and longing. I was tired and my spirit was faint, so I got up from the chair and moved to my bed. As I lay there, I held my journal close to the small candle lit at my bedside, and I scribbled away. I lamented my day of strife, confessing to the Lord my confusion over why He had me in Zambia and saying I didn't understand why I was feeling so much tension over His call to mother children.

I fell asleep as tears streamed down my cheeks and landed on my open journal. My pen still in hand, I rose a few hours later to a tender knock at the door of my heart. Only half awake, I wrote these words in my journal: "She will be entrusted to your hands. She will be placed in your arms. She will be brought to you and you will know. She will be your daughter and you will be her mother."

I woke the next morning with my journal near me. I was slightly confused but tender in spirit as I could feel my eyes burning from a night full of tears. I opened my journal and read the words I had written during the night. I began to cry. I felt the Spirit writing these same words on my heart, and in the depths of my being, I knew at that moment that I had a daughter. Somehow, somewhere, a little girl out there would someday call me Mommy. As I prayed, the name that kept coming to mind was Precious, and from that moment, I was certain that Jesus was giving me that name for her as a promise. In the fragility of that moment, joyful as it was, the agonizing cries of "Where is she? Where is my Precious?" began.

February 17, 2010

On a Wednesday morning about a week later I woke to the sound of my alarm. On weekdays, my alarm was always set for 5:59 a.m., a reminder to let the night guard go home after his twelve-hour shift. My feet hit the ground, and I had an unusual pep in my step as I walked into the kitchen and grabbed the ring of keys. I pawed my way through them, first finding the one to open the door and then identifying the two for the padlocks on the barred gate. The guard handed me a blue pen and his notebook where each morning I left my signature, and then he placed it on the plastic chair beside the barred gate. He reached for his bag and tied it on the back of his aged bicycle, and we walked out to the twelve-foot gate. I opened the lock, thanked him, and said good-bye.

I watched him ride down the dirt road a bit and then turned, locked the gate, and went back inside. I made my way straight to the kitchen where my usual apple-and- peanut-butter breakfast awaited me. I searched for the serrated knife and quickly decided that a dull knife would work just this once. I was hungry. I realized my last meal had been a few days before. Those days had been hugely emotional. For some reason, though, I felt different after acknowledging the promise of a daughter whose whereabouts were completely unknown to me. I felt a new and beautiful sense of purpose and peace. A new drive filled my being, and my spirit was willing to let go. The previous week I had felt the weight of a responsibility that the Lord had not given me, to find my daughter. Something on this morning had caused a dramatic shift—a reminder that just as I believed He had spoken, she would be placed in my arms. I didn't have to go looking. I just had to wait with patient endurance.

I sat down on the familiar sunset-colored chair and bit into my apple slices. I had cut them thick, so with each bite the juice was sweet and full, delightful to my taste buds. The peanut butter tasted smooth and rich, though I'm sure it was chalky and dry. I was hungry, though, so it didn't matter. I opened my Bible and laid it beside me. I don't remember what I opened it to, but I knew immediately that Jesus was doing something deep in my heart. His new mercies were evident. I sat patient and confident before Him and affirmed, "She will be placed in my arms. She will be brought to me. I need not search or worry. I will be faithful. And You will place her in my arms." Though I felt fearful in acknowledging that I couldn't do anything to find my Precious, I laid the matter wholly before Jesus.

Nine o'clock came and women started filing in through the door. As they arrived, they immediately jumped on the sewing machines and began working on their projects. I made my home on the floor where I spent much of the time cutting and braiding material, and soon we were deep in conversation. We got carried away teaching each other

English and Nyanja and sharing testimonies and words from the Lord. We laughed and drank tea, and we discussed happenings within the ministry. The women decided it was time to give me a Zambian name, and they bickered and laughed as they discussed potential names. After about half an hour, one woman stood and declared, "I am the winner, so I am now your Mum. I name you Lelato, which is a Lozi name meaning 'love.' Lelato Mundia, my daughter." All the women cheered and clapped, laughed and sang.

The rest of the morning flew. I had a smile across my face, honored that I would be given a name meaning, "love," or as one woman said, "love with no restraint."

∞

I said good-bye to the women and looked at my watch. It was a quarter past 14:00, and I was tired but filled with awe. I couldn't stop thinking of what an honor it was to have been given a Zambian name by a Zambian woman who now thought of me as her child, let alone to be given the name Lelato. As I hopped into a taxi, I thought of the tiny children I was about to visit, and I meditated on showing love with no restraint. I hadn't forgotten about the promise of my Precious, but my need to be in the know had been tenderly lifted, and my spirit remained surrendered as I made my way to the orphanage.

I quietly walked through the barred door and gently shut it behind me. I felt the Spirit nudge me to go to the room where the critically sick children were. I tiptoed through the hallway and removed my shoes, placing them on a small mat. I noticed a sign above the mat that said "No Photographing!" and I opened the door and entered the room. Cribs lined the walls with small children residing in each one. A dark green contraption hung from the ceiling, and a nurse and a caregiver were weighing children. To my right were cribs for the tiniest orphans, each with a small piece of masking tape marked with a child's name. My spirit began to ache.

One of the caregivers harshly placed a child in the scale's green receiving bag, and I watched her emaciated legs dangle through the openings. Her frame tipped the red pin on the scale to 3.02 kilograms, which I knew to be around six and a half pounds. The caregiver then pulled the child out and set her on the hard floor. Too fragile to hold herself up, she fell backward and her head slammed on the tile. The caregiver swung her up by a single arm and brought her to me as she gave weak but piercing cries. I reached out to take her, and I drew her near to my body. My spirit cringed as I held her tiny frame, knowing she was much older than what her weight might have led me to believe. I walked back and forth, gently rocking her, and I gazed deep into her eyes. I asked the Lord about her, wondering what words He would give me to speak over her. I declared, "Her plight, Lord, I am willing to bear."

A caregiver soon approached me with a bottle to feed this little one. She warned me, "This one, she is refusing." She said that the baby had been brought to the orphanage recently and that she was very sick. The woman also said that the baby was between eight and nine months old. Oh, my heart.

I tried to feed her. My attempts yielded nothing except screaming, and though I didn't want to let her go, the caregiver pulled her out of my arms. She sat down on the floor with her and forced the nipple into her mouth, milk spilling everywhere as the baby thrashed. Another caregiver brought a cup in which to pour the milk and a small blanket to tie around the baby's neck as a bib. They sat the baby down and forced her mouth open, placing the cup between her lips. As the baby writhed and refused to drink, another caregiver struck the child's neck in an attempt to trigger a swallow. "No, please! I can try again! Don't hit her!" I said as I reached for her.

"No, she has to eat! And she refuses!" the caregiver said, angered.

After ten minutes or so of using their hands to chop at the child's neck in hopes that she would eat, the caregiver who had taken her from me gave up in frustration. She lifted the baby forcefully and carelessly by one arm and handed her back to me. My heart sank as her tiny frame landed in my arms, but I decided that for the rest of the afternoon, I would hold this child and be intentional in seeking Jesus's heart for her.

I interceded and declared in the Spirit the heart of Jesus over this sweet baby girl. My mind never wandered, focusing only on the opportunity to love her well. Despite the sobriety of my spirit, I couldn't forsake the reality that this child, who was destined for unrestrained love, had been deliberately placed in my arms. I left that day singing my thanks to God, who so graciously had given me a few hours with such a beautiful child.

∞

Natotela had my heart from the moment she was placed in my arms. She was tiny and broken but stunning and gentle. I often would fall asleep at night crying for her, aching to be her mother. Truly though, it never seemed reasonable to assume that she could someday be mine. As the months passed, my visits to see her became more frequent. I couldn't bear the thought that she had no one. I would often come home and write letters to her on small pieces of paper or write prayers over her in my journal. The letters were always beautiful, full of desire and pursuit, and I ached for those words to be marked on her heart. I had no idea of her situation or of the trauma and tragedy that had left her orphaned, but I knew my love for her was not in vain. My longing for her was no romantic wish or fleeting desire. My pursuit of her heart wasn't just a twenty-year-old woman's idea of a cute adventure. It was nothing of the sort. It was something deeply seeded in the will of God, which would never be thwarted.

On June 10, 2010, I rose in the morning and sat down on the sunset-colored chair where I always sat. Throughout the previous months, I had struggled daily to surrender Precious to Jesus, and though Natotela was always on my mind and had quickly become the deepest ache my heart had ever known, never did I anticipate what Jesus was going to do. With all naiveté I scribbled away in my journal, "Good morning, Jesus. Yesterday was so long, oh so long. I loved my time at the orphanage with Natotela. Thank You for her. Thank You for calling into existence the time we had. Thank You for letting me cradle her to sleep. Thank You for letting me feed her nshima … oh it was lovely. Jesus, she is beautiful. Jesus, she is precious."

And in that very moment, as I wrote, "Jesus, she is precious," it was as if the heavens opened up and I could see Him smiling over me. In the depths of my spirit I knew He was speaking to me. Not only was she precious. She was *my* Precious.

It took me hours to pick myself up off of the cold tile floor. My violent sobs were mixed with wordless groans and worshipful silence. I was shocked and uncertain but filled with complete joy and confidence. I feared my youth and the reproach that would come my way yet again, but I reveled in the honor that it was to be promised this child as my daughter. I couldn't understand why the Lord had chosen me to be her mother, but I knew it was His choosing and not mine. I waited soberly in prayer as I delighted in His majesty, and I began thinking of ways to make even more visits to the orphanage.

About a week later when I was finally over the initial shock, I made an appointment with the social worker at the orphanage office to discuss Natotela's case. I planned to inform her of my interest in pursuing adoption but knew I would need to be humble in my approach. I wasn't entirely sure how the process worked in Zambia, and I had no idea if doors would even be open to a twenty-year-old woman. Of course, since I was certain that Jesus was the author of this, I knew it would happen. It had already been established before the foundations of the earth. But I also knew that it would take time and a miracle.

The day came for my first meeting with the social worker, and I waited patiently in the small foyer of her office. A secretary typed with her pointer finger in front of me while my nerves multiplied and ferociously coursed through my body. The Zambian sun poked through the doorframe, leaving a small triangle of warmth on my foot. I prayed that Jesus would have His way and that He would fill me with unswerving belief.

"Sophie?" a woman in the back called. "You can come through." I quietly stood and headed down the hallway. We entered a small office and I sat down on a wooden chair. She closed the door behind us and sat at the desk in front of me.

"Hello," I said. "How are you?"

"Fine, thank you. And you?"

"I am also fine, thank you," I responded politely.

"You have come to discuss with me a child?" she asked, filing through papers distractedly.

"Well, yes, sort of," I said, a bit taken aback by her tone.

"They told me the one you have been visiting, but no, for that one her case is closed," the woman said bluntly.

"Okay," I said, disappointed and confused. "So what does that mean?"

"It means her case is closed. There can be no adoption."

With that I stood, completely overtaken by shock, and responded, "Okay, thank you." And I walked out, horribly sad.

I made my way to the room where Natotela was kept, placing my shoes on a small mat. I dropped my purse on the floor and quietly entered the room. I approached the crib where Natotela's name was written, and there she was: my daughter. Her eyes were wide open and her tiny frame looked nearly lifeless. I scooped her up in my arms. Then I sat down with my back against her crib and brought her right up to my chest. For the first time I held this child with absolute certainty that she was my daughter. Despite what the social worker had just said, I knew that Jesus's word was truer. Holding back my tears and ignoring my deep disappointment that stung so deep, I gazed at the beauty of my daughter as she rested and fell asleep in my arms.

About an hour passed when a nurse whom I had grown to like came through the door. I hadn't seen her yet that morning, and I was thankful she was there. In previous months I had noticed the quality of the care she gave the children. She was gentle and humble, quiet and compassionate. I appreciated the consistency of her care, and she inspired me. As she walked across the center of the room she made eye contact with me and smiled. She proceeded back to the desk where she normally sat to prepare medicines and bottles for the babies. A few moments later I heard her voice. "Sophie?"

"Yes, Mum," I said as a way of respecting her.

"Come."

I carefully stood up with Natotela still in my arms and walked over to her desk. "Last night I was praying for you. In the night very late, by zero one or even zero two, I was praying that you should be the mother to this one. I was praying and I just couldn't stop praying. God can make you the mother to this one."

In utter disbelief I quietly responded, "Thank you."

"I should keep praying until you become the mother," she said tenderly.

I don't remember if words completely escaped me or if I was able to thank her again, but I turned and sat back down with my back to the crib. This tiny girl in my arms truly was my Precious. I didn't have a clue how it was going to happen, but Jesus in His goodness was even keeping one of the nurses up in the wee hours of the morning to contend for me to be Natotela's mother. As if she hadn't already said enough to sow such real hope into my spirit, when Natotela awoke, the nurse whispered, "Natotela, your mother is here. Your mother is here. Shh, baby. Your mother is here."

∞

I continued visiting Natotela as often as I could over the many months that followed. Ministry was intensely busy, and so for the most part, my visits were limited to once, maybe twice a week. Every night before going to sleep I would lie in my bed, contending for my Precious, aching for her. I hadn't told anyone the specific word that I believed the Lord had given me and the promise He had spoken that she was my daughter, so I feared that my belief would be susceptible to my wavering emotions. However, even when my emotions ran rampant and became unpredictable, my belief was unshakable. I knew that the Lord's mercy had found me and that He would preserve me so I could continue to walk in the fullness of faith so as to receive the inheritance He had promised. He assured me over and over that no purpose of His could be thwarted (Job 42:2) and that He would yield His glory to no other (Isaiah 42:8).

This season of waiting was hugely stretching. So much about the promise of Natotela lingered and caused my being to ache, affecting every aspect of my life. My secret place with Jesus changed as He began to cultivate in me the heart of a mother, beginning with intercession. I was intensely committed to approaching the throne on behalf of Natotela—not just for her case to be opened but also for her character, her heart, and her destiny. I pleaded with the Lord morning after morning and night after night, asking for a prophetic word for her life. My spirit longed to have even just one word to declare over her life day after day, and I was overjoyed at the thought of hearing whispers from Jesus about her. Day in and day out I asked, "Jesus, would You give me a prophetic word over my daughter that I might declare into existence the harvest of glory You have destined for her?" On January 25, 2011, He responded to my heart's request in Isaiah 61:3: "And provide for those who grieve in Zion—to bestow on them a crown of beauty instead of ashes, the oil of joy instead of mourning, and a garment of praise instead of a spirit of despair. They will be called oaks of righteousness, a planting of the Lord for the display of his splendor."

Natotela would be called a mighty oak, a planting of the Lord for the display of His splendor. It was beautiful and preciously fitting. She truly was a mighty oak, strong and tender. And it was already clear that her life was a living display of His splendor.

As February passed a feeling of urgency stirred within me, signaling a coming breakthrough. As this feeling intensified, I began to experience fear for the first time in a way I would not have expected.

The stakes were rising.

The more real God's promise of Natotela became to me, the more I had to gain. But if I had heard Him wrong, or if His promise to me wasn't real, shame would fasten itself to me like a harness and hedge me in.

I would lose everything.

One evening in early March, the Spirit prompted me to stay up and to pray for Natotela's case. Though I didn't know the circumstances surrounding her situation, I prayed that her case would open up. The whole of me ached as I humbly declared what I didn't still fully believe, and I felt the shame and the guilt of unbelief seize my spirit. "Jesus!" I pleaded. "Open Natotela's case!"

I fell asleep around 3:00 a.m. The next morning I awoke from a vivid dream. In the dream one of the social workers called me on the phone and said Natotela's case had opened up. The dream was simple, quick, and clear. I checked the clock as it neared 6:00 a.m., and I got on my face again before Jesus. I needed all wisdom and discernment. I hadn't actually received a phone call, and I wasn't entirely sure if I was supposed to wait or actually go. Though I felt I was hearing His voice say "Go," I hesitated. My fear of being put to shame was crippling.

After a few hours, my spirit steadied, and I felt peace about going. I got dressed and put on sandals since I knew I'd need to run the first mile before reaching a taxi stand. I drank a glass of water and then reached in the small pocket of my bag and found one last piece of gum. I placed it in my mouth, and with that I unlocked the door, opened the screen door, and charged out. I ran along the long dusty road and then jumped in a taxi. *Precious, I'm coming*, I kept saying to myself. *Natotela, Mommy is coming.*

About half an hour later I made it to the orphanage. I was careful to wipe away my sweat and to clean up a little as I walked through the gate. It was now past 9:30 a.m., so I hoped the staff members would be in their offices. I had been praying intently for the social worker's heart to have good soil for my words to fall on, but I wasn't sure. I didn't have an appointment and I didn't know what I was going to say, but I quietly walked inside. I sat down on the wooden chair before the secretary and asked her if I could speak with the social worker. She immediately said, "Yes, you may go through."

I had visited the office many times before, always with an inquiry about Natotela's case. With each visit I had left more discouraged than ever, but I hoped today would be different. I sat down and after the social worker had greeted me in a slightly annoyed tone, I got right to the point. I spilled out my heart and she listened. I spoke quickly, leaving no room for her to interrupt. I had decided that if no was going to be her answer, she'd have to say it after hearing all of my heart.

After nearly ten minutes of sharing and pouring out my heart, I finally stopped and waited for her response. She looked into my eyes and said coldly, "There is no possibility." I waited a few moments for her to offer any other words or to give me advice, but she remained silent. Then once more she said, "There is no possibility," with absolutely no compassion or care in her voice. I was heartbroken and devastated. I felt like those words had ripped out my insides.

My stomach turned violently, and without another word I placed my hands on the arms of the chairs to stand and walk out. At that moment everything in me was put to shame, but my peaceful spirit revealed quite possibly the most miraculous mantle of grace I've ever been gifted with.

Quietly I declared, "I still believe. Jesus, I still believe."

I humbly stood, slowly removing my hands from the arms of the chair. I turned toward the door without another word to the social worker. As I made my way out of the room, another Zambian woman walked toward me. I noticed her incredible beauty, but I put my head down, shamed and nearing breakdown. I didn't want to be seen. *Jesus, I still believe. I still believe*, I repeated inwardly as violent pain permeated every ounce of my being.

"Sophie, right?" the woman asked.

Taken aback and uncertain who she was, I hesitated but managed to respond, "Yes?"

"Regarding that same one, Natotela, yes?" Before I could answer, this woman (who I now know was also a social worker) poked her head into the office I had just left and scolded the other social worker. She turned back to me and in front of the other woman said, "Everything she just said is not true. Natotela's case is difficult, but her case has opened up. This can happen. Come. Come with me."

And just like that, the tables had turned.

The God who parted the Red Sea parted the waters for me, too.

∞

On March 28, 2011, the final decision was made to move toward Natotela's adoption. Five months later, on August 25, 2011, Natotela came home with me forever, and I wrote this in her journal:

> My Precious, My Mighty Oak,
>
> Little did I know today when I woke up that I would go to bed as your mommy! Little did I know that for the rest of my life I would always remember and celebrate this day. Little did I know that today I would walk with you out of the orphanage where you would never stay again. Little did I know that today you would come home with me, and forever now we are family. Oh, I am blessed.
> Natotela, you are asleep now, safe and warm in our home. You are clean, fed, and comforted; never will you be in an orphanage again. I am amazed by what the Lord has done and can only imagine what He still will do on our behalf.
> I love you, my daughter. Mommy's here, and never will I leave you.
>
> Love, Mama
>
> Jesus, I stand in awe. With tears streaming down my face, I say thank You. Thank You. Thank You. Thank You. Thank You. Thank You. Amen.

∞

Natotela's case was an incredibly unique situation due to my age and to the Zambian adoption laws requiring a prospective adoptive parent to be twenty-five years old and twenty-one years older than the child being adopted. As a mark of His power, Jesus set in motion a display of His splendor and poured out His grace upon me to endure. After eight unfavorable court hearings and an agonizing battle of four years (with absolute determination to uphold proper ethics while fighting for the best interest of my daughter), on May 7, 2015, the law was legally bypassed and Natotela's adoption was finalized. She took my last name and a new first name, Miah. Forever, gratefulness will be my banner.

Jesus is faithful to complete what He started.

His word never returns to Him void. She will be called a mighty oak, a planting of the Lord for the display of His splendor.

Part 5

INTO HIS CHAMBERS

"Let him kiss me with the kisses of his mouth—for your love is more delightful than wine. Pleasing is the fragrance of your perfumes; your name is like perfume poured out. No wonder the young women love you! Take me away with you- let us hurry! Let the king bring me into his chambers."

—Song of Songs 1:1–4

CHAPTER

COMPASSION LEADS TO MIRACLES

The desert and the parched land will be glad; the
wilderness will rejoice and blossom. Like the crocus, it
will burst into bloom; it will rejoice greatly and shout
for joy. The glory of Lebanon will be given to it, the
splendor of Carmel and Sharon; they will see the glory
of the Lord, the splendor of our God. Strengthen the
feeble hands, steady the knees that give way, say to those
with fearful hearts, "Be strong, do not fear, your God
will come, he will come with vengeance; with divine
retribution he will come to save you." Then will the
eyes of the blind be opened and the ears of the deaf
unstopped. Then will the lame leap like a deer, and the
mute tongue shout for joy. Water will gush forth in the
wilderness and streams in the desert.

—Isaiah 35:1–6

I unbuckled my seat belt and hopped out of the car. Her little body,
clothed in every color of the rainbow, stood in the big wooden

doorframe, and her eyes were bright and joyful. One of her teachers stood beside her and motioned to her that she could run. I squatted down with my arms wide open, and my precious girl ran straight into them. Her small striped backpack hit the ground, and before I could get out a word she excitedly yelped, "Mommy! My plant is growing! Come and see! It's the first to come up! Everyone is saying, "Miah! Your plant is coming up! Your plant is coming up!"" I stepped back from our embrace, attempting to match her enthusiasm, "Wow, Miah! That's amazing! Show me! Show me!"

As we skipped back up to the classroom door, her teacher said, "It is true. Miah's seed is the first one up!" As we stepped into the classroom I was immediately bombarded by her friends shouting, "Miah's mom! Miah's mom! Miah's plant is growing first! Hers is coming up! Hers is coming up so tall." We turned the corner as Miah giggled over the excited affirmation from her friends, and my eyes landed on a small table where thirty little cups were basking in the sun. Children surrounded the table, and I laughed as I noticed another one of Miah's teachers seemed to be the designated overseer, making sure all the excitement didn't cause the table to topple over.

We approached the table in what almost felt like a parade, and Miah's other teacher said, "Okay, kids, let's calm down and step back so Miah can show her mom!" Miah squeezed my hand tightly and said, "Mommy, look!" She reached out with her tiny hands, crumbled soil under every fingernail, and grabbed the cup with her name on it. Sure enough, her little bean plant had broken through the soil. Miah pulled the cup near her face and peered into the clear plastic, admiring with awe her tiny harvest. As I knelt down to her level so I could look into her eyes and celebrate with her, I became a witness this wonder. The mystery and delight of this miracle of growth had completely captivated her, and rightly so. She looked up at me and said, "Mommy! Look! I was taking good care of it and making sure it was getting sun and water. And my teacher said I was very careful, and now my plant came up first."

"Miah, I am so proud of you! Wow! You've done such a good job! And now it's going to keep growing taller and taller, stronger and stronger!"

"Yeah, Mama! My teachers said it is going to get bigger and bigger like me!"

"Yes it will! I'm so proud of you, babe!" Without realizing it, my words became few as I looked into that tiny cup. As Miah giggled and gazed, I choked back tears. Though I wasn't fully processing it in those moments, my daughter's wonder and delight over the harvest of one seed provided an avenue for restoration of my unbelieving soul and reminded me of the destiny of my household. Though my current circumstances offered no evidence of the coming plenty, the tender care of my beloved Jesus would bring forth harvest from the seed sown in me.

After a few more minutes of gazing at the little plant and watching Miah gently water it and place her cup back in the sun, we made our way back through the classroom to leave. As we passed through the doorway I picked up Miah and squeezed her tightly, making sure she felt my pride and joy over her bean plant. We laughed and danced our way to the car, and as I closed the door after she had gotten in, her teacher called out, "We are so happy that Miah's bean popped up first. She really has taken so much pride in caring for her plant and has been so attentive and gentle. It seems right that hers was the first to break through the soil."

Her words pierced my heart. So mysteriously revealed in my daughter's preschool planting project, and in the words and the celebrations of her teachers and her classmates, was a promise from the Lord that breakthrough was coming, and forever Miah would be the first fruit of this harvest.

⌘

My heart is set on living every day with an active and authentic awareness of God's heart for people. After feeling the richness of His presence for the first time when I was sixteen, I remember stepping away with a new and genuine confidence. Over the years, as I continued to experience moments of deep, rich exposure to His heart and His character, deeper truths began to solidify in me. Though His beauty was overwhelming and His power left me trembling, it was the open door into His compassion toward me that signaled the beginning of a journey of seeing the miraculous in my life.

One night when I was eighteen, I lay on a concrete floor among thousands of other believers who had gathered in worship, and I experienced a revelation of Jesus's compassion for me. This wasn't a mystical encounter or a corporate tide that I was jumping on, but rather it was a few precisely quiet and liberating moments, where my entire being felt the Lord's deep care for me. I seemed to have caught a glimpse of His eyes, and in them was the truth that He saw all of me—and still wanted me. He still wanted me close to Him. Even as He looked upon my sin, His heart longed to draw me near. I could almost taste my vindication, completely undeserved but still wholly mine. I could feel the balm of His presence over my most long-standing wounds, and I knew His strong hands were gentle with me. He was robed in tenderness and patience, and my running in circles didn't annoy Him.

These moments contrasted starkly with what I felt like I had known compassion to be. Compassion as I had previously thought, was like sympathy on steroids, weeping with those who weep or lending a hand and a shoulder to cry on in a time of need. Though compassion definitely includes these things, I began to see that what I had believed about Jesus and His compassion was far from complete. He wasn't just a friend who felt bad for me or who cried with me in my need or reached out His hand to help me in a difficult season.

Jesus dove himself into the core of me and planted Himself there.

He saw the depths of my depravity and anchored Himself to my plight.

My need for compassion could never deplete Him.

I first stumbled on Isaiah 35 late one evening a few years later. I meditated on this portion of Scripture for months, asking Jesus for the grace to leap in faith, expecting each manifest expression of His compassion to lead to an invasion of the Holy Spirit, followed by a harvest of miracles. I gave myself to asking Him if I could be an administrator of His compassion to the nations, and I began daring to believe for impossible harvest. Verse 4 became my heart's desire and my commission, while verse 5 revealed the promise of what would happen when true compassion was manifest.

> Say to those with fearful hearts, 'Be strong, do not fear; your God will come, he will come with vengeance; with divine retribution he will come to save you.' Then will the eyes of the blind be opened, and the ears of the deaf unstopped (Isaiah 35:4–5).

The more I meditated on Isaiah 35, the more Jesus revealed other portions of Scripture that spoke to my hunger to see His compassion. Instrumental to the revelation that I needed to move in His compassion was a passage in the letter to the Ephesians, which reads, "Consequently, you are no longer foreigners and strangers, but fellow citizens with God's people and also members of his household" (Ephesians 2:19).

Though Paul did not use the word *compassion*, his accounts of what Jesus had done clearly displayed a very practical lifestyle of the compassion He moved in.

Over the course of several weeks spent looking at these verses, I felt the Lord asking me to imitate His example by bringing in strangers and making them members of my household. I went through a period of truly being awestruck and just absolutely reveling in the reality of my membership in God's household—my adoption and my daughtership. And out of that place, the revelation of my own adoption and belonging in God's family, Jesus's desire for me to move in more radical obedience in the spirit of adoption reverberated through my being. Walking out the revelation of my belonging had to look like extending compassion in a similar way that Jesus had done for me.

Though I understood completely that earthly adoption could never be a perfect representation of our eternal adoption into the kingdom of heaven, still it was beautiful. In the deepest part of me I began asking Jesus for grace to walk this out. *For the rest of my life*, I told Him, *I want to be an expression of Your compassion, a manifestation of Your faithfulness, and the fulfillment of Your promises to the orphan.*

In October 2013, I began the official adoption process again. Single, twenty-four, and still in the middle of the fight to finalize my first adoption, I was miraculously approved to adopt two more children. With Isaiah 35 as my framework, I began to dream with Jesus and to contend for miracles. It was a straightforward decision.

December 2013

I went to bed one night aching, desperate in intercession over the life of one of my precious daughters. My aching was, in part, rooted in not knowing where she was or even who she was. But tipping the scale even more was the pressing question of whether Jesus was actually going to give me this child He had promised. As I drifted off to sleep, my pillowcase dampened over my ever-increasing fear for the daughter Jesus had already birthed in my heart. In the distress of not knowing who or where she was, it was difficult for me to be still and rest knowing Jesus knew exactly who and exactly where she was.

I fell asleep crying, "Jesus, where is she? Where is my beautiful girl? O Lord, who is she? Where is she?" In my head, I knew Jesus was fully sovereign and all- knowing, but there was a great disconnect residing in the pit of my being: My heart wasn't truly convinced that it was best to relinquish control and to let His sovereignty rule. I wanted to be in the know. And though the Lord had spoken clearly and called me into a lifetime of obedience in the fields of the fatherless, I struggled to abide in biblical hope and to see prophetically what Jesus had promised.

I sat up straight, awakened from a deep sleep. I looked at my clock and it read 1:27 a.m. I immediately felt Jesus prompt me to open my Bible to Psalm 16, and when I did, my eyes instantly landed on verse 5 which says, "Lord, you have assigned me my portion and my cup; you have made my lot secure."

I knew exactly to what the psalmist's words referred. Jesus, in His kindness, awakened me in the middle of the night to share with me a word over my daughter, whom I had yet to know. When unbelief had overtaken me, He was inviting me to boldly speak back to Him His promise and to declare to my innermost being that He had indeed assigned me my portion and my cup and that my lot was secure. He was reminding me that He knew the daughter I'd call Carmel and that her placement in my family was already written in the Book of Life. In a single moment, extreme hope in His Word swallowed up my unbelief and faith emerged. As my eyes filled with grateful tears, I pulled my Bible toward my chest. And at that very moment, I saw and heard Jesus decree Carmel's final earthy adoption. My lot truly was secure.

March 2014

"No," she told me. "As long as I am in this office, I will never approve her adoption or any other adoption for you, though you are approved."

Miah and I had been back in Zambia for just over twelve hours.

It took everything in me to hold back the rage that filled my entire being. I had come to Zambia believing for favor, and though I knew I would have to face many more no's before the final yes, I was not expecting such an immediate and definitive no just after stepping back onto Zambian soil.

The meeting continued for probably another twenty minutes. Her words became sharp and cruel, even mocking. Anxiety stormed past my confident façade straight to my spirit. Every ounce of my being sank in fear and doubt. I hated the fact that we were back in Zambia. I hated the fact that I had been declaring favor over my adoptions when favor now seemed impossible. I hated the fact that old wounds from unanswered prayers had burst open again, and I hated the fact that the battle was still largely before me rather than behind me. I didn't feel like seeking Jesus and inviting Him into the confusion and the pain of those moments.

The devastation of my heart assaulted me and left me utterly hopeless. As I walked out of the gate, I lifted Miah into my arms, kissed her, and placed her in her car seat. I then opened my door on the driver's side and glanced at my watch. It was barely 11:00 a.m. on our first day back in Zambia, and already I was defeated.

"Mommy, are you okay?" Miah asked.

"Yeah, baby. I just need Jesus to come real close."

"Okay, Mama. I will pray for you." And in a voice so strong and clear she prayed, "Jesus, just come and get the Holy Spirit on Mommy and get her to feel better. Get your strong hands on her and the Holy Spirit to come on her and make her so she can feel better. Amen."

In response to my precious four-year-old's prayer, I let the door of my heart crack open just enough to allow the Holy Spirit to begin ministering to me. My fear was great, and I knew He wasn't coming to take it away but to join me in it. Compassion is long-suffering.

Layers of deep anxiety surfaced throughout the next few weeks as I grappled with my expectation of miraculous favor that I couldn't yet see. Favor, to me, had a timetable, and I already knew this adoption process wasn't going to happen fast enough. *I should never have asked and believed for favor*, I thought. *Miracles are for someone else, not me.* These were the lies that I fell asleep to and rose to—the lies I cradled close because it was safer to be prepared for the worst than to hope for something that would never happen.

I turned inward and buckled in shame.

Shame feels safe sometimes.

Over the next few weeks, I began to feel compassion Himself draw near, gently exposing the prison I was locking myself in. Compassion joined me in the room where I had held Him hostage to the release of miracles I had expected, and He tenderly announced there was another way. Jesus kindly reached down and exposed my fear-driven declarations, which insisted on a quick, painless display of His power. Instead, He invited me to hunger anew while waiting in the wilderness.

I was being stretched and awkwardly so. The long days waiting for what seemed like nothing had left me at an uncomfortable and vulnerable standstill. The question of favor had taken on a new dynamic, sowing the doubt I had known so intimately before. *Are You even going to give me the children You have promised? Are You ever going to open the womb of my heart and bring forth to deliver the children You told me were mine? Are You even going to finish Miah's adoption?* I recognized that though I had once been moving in faith, I was now moving in entitlement. I thought I deserved God's faithfulness in this adoption process. In my pride and arrogance, I truly believed that I was entitled to the miraculous and that I deserved to have Him give me my children.

I was wrong, and I knew it. But it was easier to lean into shame.

Shame sometimes pretends to nurture us.

Though my heart was set on a series of miracles that put me and my children back on a plane after an easy and beautiful few months, God was set on a miracle that could only come from looking at Him wholly and rightly in this war's waiting room, long as it may be.

∞

One day in April 2014, I got a message that left me encouraged but even more vulnerable than before.

"When I was praying for you I saw a stroller like a jogging one that people push their children in when they run. It had three wheels, one in front and two in back. It was a two-seater. I think this had something to do with twins specifically, which is why it was a two-seater. But ask Papa because the twin part I'm not exactly sure about."

I read these words over and over, asking, *Can it be? Can it really be? Lord, are you going to give me twins?* My heart leapt out of my chest, though I was quick to silence the newly triggered hope in an attempt to protect myself. For a few days, I poured over these words and beseeched the Lord for something, anything, to confirm this word was of Him. But as fear-stricken as I was, I tethered my heart to the dungeon of disbelief and refused to allow myself to think about the possibility. It would hurt too much to believe for twins, ask for them, and then walk in expectation of God's favor again. But despite my efforts to tie down my longing heart, I couldn't shake the possibility of twins. I became terrified because now, instead of favor being on a timetable, it was on a twintable. I felt like I had no control as I again made corrupt assumptions about God's favor and held Him hostage to what I was now expecting—twins.

Two days later, my phone rang and my social worker's name appeared on the caller ID. Loveness didn't normally call, but I had been trying to get in touch with her for a week. She had sent me a text the day before saying she would call soon, which happened to be this morning. She obviously didn't have much time, so she got right to the point.

"Sophie, I have found children to place with you. I was discussing their case with my coworkers today, and it looks like they are cleared for adoption. I will need to verify their background with the director at the orphanage, but I am going that side tomorrow anyway." I was stunned at what she was saying, because normally Zambian social workers never call with news like this.

"Children?" I said, emphasizing the plural.

"Yes, call me by 14:00 hours tomorrow. But for now at least, it's two girls who are twins. Call me tomorrow." Then the phone disconnected. I thought it must have been a dream. I didn't have the chance to say but a single word, and just like that, twin girls were a possibility. I threw myself on the floor and wept in gratitude. Surely, Jesus was doing this. He was going to place twins in my family—in perfect alignment with the prophetic word I had been given. I could hardly contain myself.

The clock couldn't tick fast enough as the next thirty-six hours dragged on. My head felt like it was in the clouds, and a smile was plastered across my face. I desperately wanted to tell everyone at home, but I knew it was wisdom to wait. I knew there was a possibility that my social worker could call back with news that the twins were not adoptable, but I couldn't imagine that. *Surely it won't happen like this*, I thought.

I called Loveness the moment the clock on my phone showed 14:00 hours, and the social worker picked up the phone. "Ah, Sophie. I haven't yet been to the orphanage to see the children, but I discussed this on the phone with the director. He said we could just check at the district office where they came from, but from what he knows they don't have anyone. But we can go now. I'm sure if you can be ready, you can just come and meet the girls. I am already getting transport for another issue, so you will find me there." Five minutes later Miah and I were in the car on the way to the orphanage. I was ready to meet the twins whom I believed would soon be my daughters. What a miracle!

The moment I laid eyes on them, an overwhelming awe and wonder came over me. *These are the children I've been praying for*, I told myself. *These are my girls. Though I've never seen them before, their hearts are bound to mine. These are the ones whose grief has stricken me and whose pain I will forever carry.* They were identical and beautiful. Their huge eyes were filled with hopelessness so raw, and their gaze was empty. Their fourteen-month-old frames were famished and their cheeks sunken low. They rocked themselves back and forth in their cribs, attempting to numb the pain of having no one. More than most children I have met, these two precious girls knew they were alone. Oh, if only they could see how Jesus was authoring their stories. If only they knew whom He had just brought into the room.

For nine days we continued bonding, visiting for several hours each day as we moved toward legal custody and their discharge from the orphanage. With each moment Miah and I were able to spend with Tamanda and Jenala, our relationship became sweeter and sweeter. Miah started to get giggles out of both of them, though Tamanda more easily than Jenala. The sound of those three giggles kept me awake at night, lost in worshiping a God of true miracles. Though stepping into a new normal as a single mother of a four-year-old and two fourteen-month-olds would be difficult beyond measure, I was ready. These precious twins were going to be part of our family, and the testimony of God's miraculous redemption was already on my tongue.

"Sophie, everything is good for the twins except we just need to make final confirmation with the district because that is the village where they originally came from. There is one social worker who was there when they first came when their mother was still alive, so that lady will be the best person to see about getting the proof of their orphan status and about getting police reports and death certificates for the parents."

"Okay," I said. "Do you want me to go there, or are you going to?"

"If you can manage you can go. I won't be able to leave the office, and I will be in court tomorrow, and we have different programs the rest of this week. If you can manage, I will call that same lady and tell her you are coming to discuss. Her name is Ms. Sakala."

I jumped in the car a few hours later and headed out to the town, which was close to the village where the twins had first come from. After the long drive, I reached the small social welfare office, painted a grayish coral color, and entered the building. There were three people in the single-room office, one reading a newspaper and the other two looking through a stack of files on the floor. I sat down in a chair near the door and waited for about ten minutes. None of them seemed the least bit interested in acknowledging that I had walked into their office.

"Excuse me," I said hesitantly. "I am looking for Ms. Sakala. Is she here?"

"It's me," said one woman who was digging through files. "What do you want?"

"Did Loveness call you?" I asked.

"Yes. She called. Now there is no use in discussing because the twins are not adoptable."

"What? I don't understand. Everything Loveness has told me has been about how the girls are double orphans and no one is coming for them. Is there a relative who is going to come and get them from the orphanage?"

"No, they are orphans. No one is coming for them. But the problem is that there is no file. It is lost, so they won't be going for adoption."

"Who brought them in the first place?"

"The mother did just before she passed." After a pause, she added, "But there is no more discussing. Since I don't have the file there is nothing I can do."

She stared blankly at me without another word.

I felt the presence of the Lord come upon me and usher me out of the office. I was speechless. I made it to my car before my knees buckled and I fell into the driver's seat. Tears streamed down my face as I pulled out onto the main road, and a plague of confusion swept over me. I dialed Loveness's number and explained to her what Ms. Sakala had just said.

"I am sorry, Sophie. She told me the same."

"Did that just happen?" I cried. "Are Tamanda and Jenala really going to be in an orphanage until they age out, because someone misplaced their file? Was she just saying that looking for a bribe? This is precisely the plight of the fatherless that no part of me can tolerate. I cannot tolerate this. Where is justice for these two?" I couldn't control the heaving that came upon me. I pulled my car over to the side of the road and stayed there for a while.

I made it home later that night after picking up Miah from a friend's house, and I managed to keep myself together long enough to tuck her into bed. We read books and snuggled tightly under the covers, and I kissed her forehead sweetly. I smiled and giggled with her, but my insides were overwhelmed. As we prayed, she whispered to Jesus, "I am hoping for my sisters and that they are going to come home. Jesus, help them to get home from the orphanage so they can be in our family and not be sad and have no mommy anymore. And that they can have a big sister because I am sad for them because I know what it is like when they don't have a mommy. Amen." I tucked her in, told her I loved her more than she could ever imagine, and made my way out to the little sitting room.

The hours that followed will forever be a tangible memory to me. It's difficult even now to describe what happened because the intensity of those hours is unmatched by most experiences I've ever had. I was screaming and crying and punching the floor. I was bursting with love for Jesus down to the tip of my toes, even laughing at times. I felt confusion like a plague and freedom like a wide-open sky. Surging anger and rest came over me at once, both expressions of surrender in worship. This was new intimacy with Jesus and a greater revelation of His heart of compassion. I couldn't pretend that my heart for Tamanda and Jenala was more compassionate than His. I had to let these moments hurt. I had to be willing to sit in this exposure to such brutal realities, knowing that these very moments would fuel my fire and intensify my hunger for justice.

Why, O Lord? Why? I couldn't wrap my mind around the injustice. I couldn't end my fight for these children and surrender to an injustice so cruel, to wickedness so perverse. I wrote in my journal,

> O Lord, Tamanda and Jenala are going to grow up in an orphanage, labeled forever as double orphans, because one woman lost their files and doesn't care to do anything? O Lord, how? Even if it's not with me, how can these children never be given a chance to have a family?
>
> What are You going to do for these children? I cannot do anything outside of You. I am helpless. Oh this plight—how? How to bear this cup I know not—only bear it with me. Teach me Your ways. Let me see deliverance. Jesus, I am angry. These children! I hate injustice. It is not okay. I weep for them. I rip my clothing. I hate this for them. Though I am so confused, never let me insulate this pain or create some explanation in my mind to make this "in Your will" for them. I don't want false theology to pacify me in my confusion. I don't want anything to do with "all in God's timing" clichés or "He won't give you what you can't handle." Jesus, I know this injustice is not Your will for Tamanda and Jenala. Only let me burn even more to see justice brought forth, and in my burning, I declare:
>
> You will find that I have loved You, Lord. I have loved You hard and with abandon. My eyes are on You, locked in. I'm gazing. You will find me fully and wholly in love with You. I will drink this cup—this double agony, this double grief, this searing pain, this deep anger, and this hatred of injustice—because of them. They are beautiful. They are worth it. And I will love You wholly as I drink this cup. Sowing in tears. Sowing in tears. Sowing in tears.

Those few hours on that hard wooden floor brought me to a breakthrough that was right then miraculously released. I didn't realize it at the time, but I had stumbled upon a wide-open passage into the heart of God where His compassion was tangible. I realized that His fierce zeal for justice is true because His heart of compassion is true first. There is no room to believe otherwise.

I will never claim to operate fully out of God's heart of compassion, but I am certain that on this night He invited me to partner with Him in His compassion and in His ache to see justice done for Tamanda and Jenala. It felt natural for me to suffer in those moments, simply because something deep had solidified in me that they were worth it and that a miracle was happening. Though it made no logical sense, I began to believe that compassion really does lead to miracles. Tamanda and Jenala were worth surrendering myself and my desire to be their mother. They were worth the pain of seeing their plight—even if in the natural realm there was nothing I'd ever be able to do besides weep for them. They were worth it. And so was the Lord. And the intimacy I knew with Him right there began to expose a miraculous work that He was doing in me, the last place I'd been looking for a miracle.

I went to bed that night unconcerned about the plight of my family and about my circumstances. I laid my head on my pillow, thanking the Lord for His word that promised miracles were coming, even if we couldn't see them. Though grief was my portion as I pleaded for the twins and refused to pacify myself with protective theology, I drifted into sleep with the knowledge that God's compassion would yield miracles despite what I could see. I slept soundly, wrapped tenderly in His care, which was working miracles in my depths.

For the first time since I had set out on this adoption journey again, I let go of expectations. I wasn't giving up and I definitely wouldn't stop contending for a miraculous breakthrough, but something was different. Next to the miracle that I was experiencing in those moments of intimacy with the Lord, a miracle in circumstance hardly felt like a priority anymore.

Believing I had a right to things outside of grace had opened the door for me to take offense. But in the following hours, I started to understand that this season was kindly and precisely purposed by Jesus to ensure that I be restored to poverty of spirit. I did not like working through the offense that entitlement had allowed, and how that only increased my agony over the twins' plight. But I began to grow certain that on the other side of this, I would be positioned to humbly receive what Jesus had wanted to give me all along, the very thing I had been crying out for—harvest.

My phone rang and I saw it was Loveness paging me. I picked up the phone and called her back. She didn't say much but insisted I come to her office.

I made arrangements to be at her office the next morning, first thing. I was nervous and expectant, with no idea what would happen. I thought maybe something had happened with the social worker in the village district and maybe adoption was possible for the twins. To my confusion, Loveness told me about a case that one of her colleagues had handled a week or so before. She had overheard the story being told in the office next to hers.

"This grandmother came in with a baby. She was complaining that she was very sick and that her arm was paining and that she couldn't manage to keep this infant safe in her surroundings. There is no one else who can keep this baby, and the baby is in danger if she stays with the grandma."

"Wow," I said hesitantly. I didn't understand why she was telling me this.

"Sophie, this same grandmother is the grandmother to Miah. She asked if the baby could go with you and be raised with the sister or else the baby would die. The baby is in the orphanage now and she is sick and too small."

All I could think about was the prophetic word about the stroller that my friend had sent me and how there was one wheel in front and two in the back. My mind calmed as I whispered under my breath, "From one womb, two children. Two from one womb. Miah the first fruit."

"Oh my," I said, completely overwhelmed. "Yes, Loveness. Of course."

∞

On July 12, 2014, I put Miah in the car and we went to visit her sister at the orphanage for the first time. Eleven days later, on July 23, 2014, my nearly one-month-old baby girl of the same womb as Miah came home forever. I wrote this in her journal:

My Beautiful Harvest!

> You are home! Forever part of our family! You are tiny and precious and perfect in every way. Mommy and Miah are smitten. We love you, baby girl.
> Oh Jesus, this is harvest. This is compassion that leads to miracles. This is divine. Thank You, Lord. I have no words.
> The miracle that happened today, Jesus, is such a mark of Your character. You are sovereign. You are all-knowing. You are humble. You are faithful. Thank You for my beautiful Carmel. Home at last. Glory. Hallelujah. Amen.

∞

My assumptions about what God's favor should look like in this season were wildly mistaken. Time was not the indicator of how much favor had been poured out; neither was a gift of twins or of an infant with biological ties to my first daughter. The truest favor lavished on me was intimacy with Jesus as He tenderly responded to my searing doubts and to my entitled heart with His rich and undying compassion. Unanswered prayers and deep grieving launched me into His zealous heart of justice and invited me to engage with Him in the places of my greatest confusion. His loving kindness attended to my broken and corrupt beliefs about who He was and about what He had for me and gently restored me to hope anew in the harvest He had promised.

165

As I look back now and consider this specific season of my life, I return to Isaiah 35. The miracle of God's compassion is so wild and life-giving. He is so dramatically invested in taking our ashes and making us beautiful. His interest and commitment to tenderly shepherd my heart through the confusion and the aching had led to a miracle in me, not just a miracle in my circumstances. Had the twins been given to me or had tiny Carmel never been given to me, still the miracle was being worked in me. No longer would I need to search for circumstantial evidence of His goodness. Instead, I could feel that He was sewing Himself into the very fabric of me so that I could come alive in receiving the miraculous that He had been doing all along.

Circumstance could no longer dictate my response to Jesus and to His compassion. No longer did I see injustice as a place where His compassion was absent. Rather, I was learning that injustice has no power to disarm Jesus of anything, especially of compassion. Though His justice may not always been seen, and it may never make sense why perverse evils seem to prevail so much of the time, still I will choose to engage with Him and to declare the deep, hidden miracles. In unanswered prayers I will heed the invitation to partner with Him, knowing that all of His authoring is penned in compassion and He will always speak the final word.

A fundamental truth began to emerge confidently in me: in all that is barren, He will, in due time, yield His harvest.

The desert and the parched land will be glad.

His compassion always leads to miracles.

CHAPTER 17

A CARRIER OF STORIES

I caught a glimpse of her from behind wearing that red bandana over one shoulder and under the other. Like a mama wearing a *chitenge* to hold her young, so she stood, eyes on the horizon and the dry Zambian dust beneath her. Her hands grasped the corners of the bandana and pulled them tightly across her chest, securing a knot. Her tiny shoulders carried the weight of an empty plastic water bottle that she pretended was a baby, while her precious heart carried the weight of all that she longed for. She had figured out sometime in her six years that if she couldn't have a mama, then at least she could be one. Even if it was just to an empty water bottle.

She walked quietly, every once in a while patting the bottom of the water bottle as a mama would pat her baby's bottom. She sang tender songs as her eyes drifted off to the sky, somehow holding on to that tiny thread of hope that a mama would come for her someday. She gently brought her baby underneath her arm and around to the front and later kissed her on the cheek. She spoke quiet words of love into her ear and held her close.

Kids who were passing by began pointing and laughing at her. She knew they had witnessed her kissing the cap of a water bottle and pretending it was a baby, so she put her head down and began walking in the opposite direction. Then she leaned her head down and ever so gently kissed the top of the water bottle again.

Because where the world saw no worth, she saw otherwise.

What no one else wanted, she called her own.

∽

I met Niza in 2009 when she was around six years old. She had just been placed in an orphanage, and the transition was clearly difficult for her. She was withdrawn and quiet, and her eyes screamed of a stunning innocence that had been maliciously hijacked from her. In my spirit I could feel a weight of grief over her life that was incredibly daunting, while simultaneously everything in me knew that I needed to pursue her heart. She needed someone to love her, someone to hold her, and someone to kiss her cheek just as she did to her sweet water-bottle baby. Truly, she had learned so much about love from her lack. But learning from our lack goes only so far.

Over the next few years, I continued to consistently visit the village where she lived, and I let her know each time that I would be back to see her. Some days I would surprise her outside of her school and walk her back to the orphanage. Other times I would come and help her and the other children do their chores. Over time and in the kindness of Jesus, Niza began to find safety and warmth in me, and her walls began to fall. She began to point to pictures of us that I had printed for her, saying, "Mama Sophie loves me. Jesus give Mama Sophie to me for love. Jesus love me. Jesus love me so much."

One night, about a month after I had been visiting her almost every day, I wrote in my journal,

> We're playing and I hear her small voice say, "Let's go there."
> Her finger points to a desolate place along the far side of the
> wall. I walk toward the home and scrunch up my body against
> the red-dirt bricks. She wiggles her little limbs to find the perfect
> place, and I hold her. In the cool Zambian eve, I wrap up her bare

arms in mine, protecting her from the cold. Her head rests gently against my chest and I breathe deeply.

As I hold her I cannot imagine what she is thinking. I cannot fathom the pain she once knew and the pain she still knows. I wonder what this moment means to her. I wonder what it's like to be her age with no one, alone in this big place.

Her tears begin to fall, silent and steady. She pulls her head away from my chest to look into my eyes. She stares, but her gaze is empty. I smile gently and her eyes blink, causing another tear to fall. Her life wounds me, but none of this is about me. I kiss her on her forehead.

She puts her head back against my chest, this time just over my heart. Her quiet tears keep falling, dampening my shirt below. Tears also begin to fall from my eyes as the darkness of the night presses in. I know it's now time to say good-bye, but why?

The graciousness of God met me in those nights as I found it difficult to take her back to the orphanage where my love must have felt sour as she fell asleep alone. I wondered how the love of God would penetrate her little life, but I believed wholeheartedly that it would. Day and night, night and day, I stood hoping and praying that although the world judged her of no worth, she would know to whom she belonged. I began to pray fervently that Niza would know that Jesus called her His own, and I gave myself to doing all that I could to be a tangible expression of His faithfulness to her.

One day in the middle of 2012 I headed out to the village to visit Niza and upon arriving found that she was no longer at the orphanage. Scared and confused, I asked the caregivers where Niza was, and their response blew my mind.

"Someone came to pick her up. Someone just came shouting for her. They went very far from here, somewhere like one hundred kilometers from here. But we don't know who he was."

Niza was gone. Not a word more was spoken. Outside of a miracle, there'd be no way for me to trace where she was. Immediately, the fervency of my prayers over the years became obvious: Niza needed to know that Jesus called her His own, because everything in me told me that where she had just been taken was not a safe place for her.

For the next three years, I failed in all of my attempts to find Niza or to get information about who she was with. I wondered if I'd ever see her again. I cried as I penned her name in my journal, wondering whether she was safe and cared for. As I walked on the familiar land where we used to play, I'd cringe, wondering who was telling her that she was loved and who was wrapping their arms around her so she could feel it. I'd lie awake some evenings and wonder if anyone had told her that day that she was beautiful and that she belonged to Jesus. And selfishly, I cried, hoping for an opportunity to see her again just to hold her once more and to remind her how deeply she was loved.

But I wasn't wholly pure in what I hoped for. In her disappearance, I was forced to face a reality that I hated, one that revealed a deep and wild selfishness in me: I liked how it felt to love her. And now that she was gone, the only way I could love her was to pray.

I didn't want to just pray.

May 2015

It was midmorning as I made my way to the village to help out with a child assessment program. As soon as I arrived I jumped right in with the staff since nearly eighty children had to be assessed. The afternoon sun strengthened and began to warm my chilled frame, and my heart swelled with each child who passed through my station.

"Okay, are you ready?" I said gently to a group of five children. They looked back at me blankly until I repeated myself. "Are you kids ready to get started?" One little girl looked up at me and shouted, "Yes, mama! We are ready!"

"Okay, let's go then." I got the kids in a little line and had them all hold hands, and then I reached down to grab the little girl's hand. I led them outside and down to the building where the assessment process would continue, and then I turned around to make my way back to my station.

A graying Zambian man approached me, and as he neared I recognized him, though I hadn't seen him since sometime in 2013. "Moses!" I said. "Ah, Moses, is that you?"

"Ah, Sophie. How are you, my dear? It's been long!" he said, embracing me.

"Moses! Oh, I am so happy to see you. It has been so long! How are you?"

"Oh, I am fine. I am very fine and everyone is okay," he responded.

"Wow! I haven't seen you in so long! I was just thinking about you the other day because I was thinking about Niza and wondering how everyone was doing and if anyone has heard from her."

"Oh, who's this girl? Niza? Oh yes, that girl is one that you love very much. No, Niza, I haven't seen her or heard anything from her. That was some time ago that she left—2012, wasn't it?"

"Yeah," I said, disappointed. "Three years ago." My heart again felt the ache of Niza's plight and the extent to which I missed her. "Okay, well I should get going. Moses, it's great to see you. I hope that you have a nice day. Please greet your wife. And also, if you do see Niza again, can you please make sure she knows how much I love her? Please tell her that I never stop praying for her."

"Sophie, you are kind. Greet your babies for me. I am happy to see you today." With that, he walked off.

I stood still for a moment in an attempt to regain focus and to rid my mind of all the thoughts I was now thinking. Moments later I returned to the assessment room to carry on with the program, but I couldn't shake what was going through my mind.

Something is terribly wrong when a man assigned to be an earthly protector knows nothing about the daughter he has reared.

For the next few hours I continued working hard to stay present and content where I was. Though in body I was very much engaged with the children, my spirit had picked up that Jesus was doing something else and that He had brought me to the village for another reason. My interaction with Moses had caught my attention in a unique way, and I discerned something more happening in the spirit.

There was a war going on for Niza.

And somehow Jesus wanted to include me in the strategy of His victory in her life.

I made my way up the dirt path as the afternoon sun began to sink in the deep blue sky and I prayed. I wondered in all that was going on, what Niza was doing right then. I knew without a doubt that her circumstances looked grim and that her heart was being crushed under the weight of devastation. I could feel it. A tear dripped from my eye as I remembered that several years earlier her biological father had died. Another tear fell as I sighed, wondering how Moses (her papa who had cared for her for three years in the orphanage) had seemingly forgotten her. I cringed, but as I prayed I was filled with certainty that her heavenly Father knew precisely where she was. *O Lord,* I thought, *if only you would show me where she is.*

I walked through the door of my friend's home and sat down, putting my feet up on her ottoman. My girls had been playing up at her house where our most precious Auntie Idah kept them while I was working. I chatted with Idah for about an hour, and then I thanked her and headed out to pack up my girls in the car. I wanted to get home before dusk.

A few more members of the staff made their way up the path at the same time, and I asked them how their stations had wrapped up. This had been the first assessment program for some of them, and I wanted to hear their feedback. Though I had intended for our conversation to be a quick exchange, it ended up being much lengthier, landing my children and me in their house. The afternoon felt oddly drawn out, and the sun continued its way west.

"I really need to get going. I need to get the girls home and in bed."

"Yes, you have a long drive," one of them said.

"Is it okay if I use your bathroom?" I asked, prepping for the hour drive.

"Of course!"

I made my way to the bathroom and looked down at my phone. It was nearing 18:00 hours and I thought, *How did that happen? I wanted to get home before dusk.*

I managed to get the girls back in the car and we took off. I thought of Niza as I put my car into gear, still wondering where she was and if she knew how loved she was. I looked out into the mountains and felt the hugeness of Jesus press up against my smallness. Dusk had crept in close, and through a thick haze that made it difficult to see, I thought, *Why didn't I leave earlier? I hate driving at this time of day. It's so hard to see.*

My tires kicked up dust behind the car as I picked up speed down a slight hill. I noticed three tall, lean frames far ahead of me, walking in the direction of my car. As they got closer, the frame furthest on the left caught my attention. Her body moved slowly, and as I approached she lifted her head and hesitantly turned to look. Time stopped as our eyes met and locked.

I threw my car into park and jumped out, instantly weeping. She ran straight into my arms and buried herself in my embrace, sobbing in relief. I cradled her head close to my chest, hoping she could hear the heartbeat of someone who loved her fiercely. I opened my mouth to try to say a few quiet words, but nothing came out. After a few moments, I took another deep breath and tried again. I managed to whisper one thing.

"Niza."

∞

After only a few minutes she began spilling out detailed accounts of the heinous abuse she was enduring day after day. The intensity of her confiding was as if she was somehow trying to make up for the lifetime of trauma she had suffered in the last few years. Her desperate gasps for breath between sobs revealed an injustice so cruel, a plight so perverse.

As I listened to Niza and held her tall, lean frame, I couldn't believe she was twelve now. Though years had passed, she still curled herself up in my arms just as she had when she was six—back when her orphanhood was still fresh. But now there was something different. With many more years under her belt, it all felt that much weightier. She was a seasoned orphan now.

As Niza began to calm down, I slowly started to whisper true words in her ear. I told her she was brave to tell me all those things and to believe she was loved even in the face of such evil every day. I told her that though the world labeled her as an orphan and earthly circumstances rendered her one, Jesus had spoken her name and called her His own. I reminded her of the love I had for her and said she was no orphan to me. She belonged with me. I told her that she was beautiful and kind and that she had such a pure heart. I reminded her that she was safe and that Jesus had planned these moments for her to be held by me. I told her that it was okay if she wanted to just feel little, like she did when she was six, and that it was safe for her to lean into my love. And she did. She leaned in hard. When she was younger, my arms had become a haven for her where she could drop the title of orphan and rest in belonging. I was so grateful that she had not forgotten.

"I just want to be with you, Mama."

"Oh, Niza," I said, aching for her. "I want that too, babe. I've always loved you as my own."

We stayed like that for quite some time, and then I pulled out my phone. I called one of the caregivers from the orphanage where she used to stay, first so she could see Niza but then also so we could talk. She arrived about fifteen minutes later, and I briefed her while Niza played with my girls in the car.

"The abuse is too bad, Inonge."

"Yeah, I can see. She is not looking good. I don't know what can be done. We can get the social worker to go do an investigation. We have room at the orphanage."

Inonge and I continued discussing details, and she briefed me on some other history that I had not known and that Niza might not have known either.

"There is no protection for children like this, Sophie. It's too bad. But let me call Gloria and make a program. Go and get Niza."

"Okay," I replied. I walked over to my car where all three girls were giggling and smiling. Niza had always loved Miah, but she hadn't seen her since she was two years old, and she had never met Carmel. Her eyes were glowing as she played with them. *Oh, to have her in our family*, I thought. *Lord, I'm willing. I'll do anything.*

I brought Niza over to Inonge as she talked with Gloria on the phone. "Niza, can you come to the orphanage on Tuesday? We can talk with Esther and Gloria and see what we can do. It's not okay for you to be this thin and to have so many troubles. You should be free. You can't live like this."

Niza nodded, thankful. An ounce of relief showed through her eyes, and she wrapped her arms around me and leaned into my embrace. I kissed the top of her head and held her softly.

"Niza, I should escort you. Now it has become late. Let's go," Inonge said.

I kissed her forehead again. "I will see you on Tuesday," I said. "I love you forever, Niza." Tears streamed down her face again, and she looked bravely into my eyes. "I love you too, Mama," she said. "Forever." I thanked Inonge with a hug and watched them walk down the path. A whirlwind of emotions flooded my heart, but mostly I stood amazed. I couldn't believe what had just happened. I hopped back in my car and thought, *Glad I didn't make it home before dusk.*

The next few days were long as I waited for Tuesday. I regretted not asking Niza more questions, though for obvious reasons I was also glad I hadn't. I tried to piece together all the information she had shared, but there were still many gaps in Niza's story. The many layers of death, secrecy, and conspiracy were so complex that they were hard to sift through. I did what I could to map out what she had disclosed to me over the years and to write my recommendation for an investigation.

Tuesday morning finally came, and I reached for my phone to call Inonge to confirm the meeting time. She didn't pick up, so I sent her a quick message: "Meeting still happening today? What time? Page me then I can call you back." About twenty minutes later I got a message back from her: "Not 2day. Will call u."

My heart sank as I wondered what had changed. I trusted her, though, and committed to wait for her to call. I wondered what Niza was doing but rejoiced, knowing I'd get to see her in a day or so.

Wednesday evening came and my phone beeped as I was making dinner for my girls. Inonge had texted, saying, "U can call." I quickly turned down the burner on the stovetop and dialed her number, walking into my bedroom.

"Hi, Sophie. Niza didn't come. She is gone and we don't know where. Gloria came again today but there was no meeting. We think someone grabbed her to take her back. There is nothing we can do to help her now."

A million questions flooded my mind, and I lowered myself to sit on the bed. I couldn't get out any words because everything felt so familiar: the incredible reunion, the divine intervention, the tangible hope, and then the halt, with the situation unresolved. I had walked this road before with Mutinta and many others. And now I was walking it with Niza.

"Okay," I said in shock. And I hung up.

The raw and utter helplessness felt like the weightiest blow, leaving a hollow feeling in the deep of me. I was back where I started. Fighting for Niza somehow brought life to my being. I believed that somehow Jesus was bringing forth justice on her behalf, but I despised the helplessness that circumstances decreed. I wondered if that would be the last time I'd ever see her, the last time I'd ever be able to hold her close enough so she could hear my heartbeat. I yelled, "I already told you, God! I don't want to just pray." And I wept. I knew there was no deceit in God's heart and no leading of His that could end in abandonment. But it sure felt like it.

Prayer felt like an obituary, a matter-of-fact statement of another casualty.

But I knew it was time again to bind myself to what I could not see—and to let His Word dominate my experience.

∞

A sure way to find out the real character of a person is to observe them in a season when circumstances have rendered them helpless. When things are taken outside of the arenas of control we establish (often daily), we quickly see that our faith is a lot shallower than we'd like to admit.

When we are truly served prayer as our only means, we get to see a much truer picture of who we are—reluctant and unbelieving in many ways. Our flesh so naturally clings to what we can see. It's true—we all want to be home before dusk.

But on the other side of this is an incredible miracle that moves the heart of God. It's that tiny flicker of hope in the haze of uncertainty that says, "Pray again; just let Him hear your voice once more." And it's right there—in that turning of our spirit one more time back to God—where we witness just how courageous it is to pray.

A people who don't see but still believe, people willing to trust, even when nothing makes sense.

He calls us His own.

My last moments with Niza seemed to have been snatched away and erased even, as if somehow in her second disappearance, my love for her was voided. I couldn't deny the miracle of having seen her once more, but it felt like a tease. I know the heart of God and I know He'd never mock me, but it was so hard to wrap my mind around these events. This was another mystery in my journey with Him, another disappointment that I wanted to dance upon but couldn't—at least not right away.

As I walk the road of this recent sorrow, I am gentle with myself because I know God is gentle with me. I find that my disappointment causes me to bump into Him in a new and dramatically intimate way if I keep my heart from offense. My helplessness looks less like chains and more like a sweet reminder that I am not God. He causes me to wholeheartedly surrender again, and this I know is the cross. The burden feels light, and courage starts to have its way in me.

I've come a long way since the day I first set foot in Zambia, but I'm not there yet. In the last several years Jesus has taught me that beauty rising from ashes is a lifetime, and crowning children in beauty is a process.

He has taught me that the most courageous thing that I can do is to carry the stories of the brokenhearted and to do the work of intimacy with Him right there. I've learned that just stepping into the pain of the fatherless, without a guaranteed miracle or visible resolve, requires bravery unmatched. And I've learned that if there is anywhere in the world I want to be, it is with Jesus among the broken. What the world does not value I choose otherwise.

Niza taught me a lot about being brave. She taught me a lot about the courage of leaning into love. But most important, her life reminds me to keep carrying stories. For there will be no greater day than the day I stand face to face with Jesus and the crumbled stories I've been carrying through this life, land their ears on his chest. For justice is the heartbeat of our King, and every son and every daughter will meet a heavenly resolve in Him.

He is the one who will crown us in beauty.

Forever.

Epilogue

My Beautiful Jesus,

Let not my spirit grow proud of this season now behind me. Let not my revelation grow stale, for I cannot be sustained by the bread of yesterday. Let not my heart expect You to do what You did in my former days. Behold, You are doing a new thing.

Oh, that I may never weary in the work of intimacy. Belonging to You. Delighting in You. Being wholly Yours. Sitting with You. Knowing You. Listening to You. Forever that I may be authentic with You in the secret.

Beloved, this is all from You, for You, and to You. Beloved, have Your glory. You are altogether lovely, altogether worthy of my life so small. Thank You for the way You have loved me, so patiently and so fiercely. Your shepherding of my heart is my greatest joy. Thank You for giving me all of Yourself, for not hiding Yourself from me. Your love has marked me forever.

That I might go on in loving You, Jesus, this is my deepest plea. That I might walk as if You were my only love, forever first without confusion of priority. Jesus, that You might carry me through the troubles of this life, fixing my gaze on You and keeping me with You. Jesus, You have loved me so well. You make me come alive, and it is my greatest prayer that I may love You well in return all of my days and that You will find at the end of this life, that I have loved You and haven't turned my face from You. Jesus, I press on in knowing You. You are my joy.

Your goodness is like no other. Your faithfulness more true than any. You are kind to me. You are the very breath I breathe. I am proud to be Yours. Yes, I am so proud to see my need for You. Keep me poor in spirit, my Lord.

Behold, You are doing a new thing. Let me forever though, be a constant carrier of Your heart for the fatherless. And though there will be grief and a long-suffering true, Your victory is sure, so let Your strategy be my joy.

I love Your heart.

Thank You for giving it to me in such purity and strength.

You blow my mind, Jesus.

I smile because I know You.

Forever yours,
Me

READERS' GROUP DISCUSSION GUIDE

Chapter 1
Yes

1. How does the Lord speak to you? Do you know when He is speaking to you?
2. Are you avoiding the Lord's call in any areas of your life? Would things be different if fear weren't involved?
3. What is the freshest surrender in your life, and how have you seen fruit in your obedience? What aspect of God's character is closest to you in times of deep surrender?
4. Jesus tells us in the book of John, "Whoever has my commands and keeps them is the one who loves me" (John 14:21). Have you made that connection in your spirit, recognizing that obedience is a testimony of love? Do you experience conviction, encouragement, or both as you ponder this truth?

Chapter 2
The Hardest Conversation

1. Has your decision to follow Jesus ever caused division in your family or your community? How did that division affect your relationship with Jesus and your willingness to press on in obedience?
2. Can you think of a time when a family member or a friend confided in you about something Jesus was saying and you immediately were confused and scared? How do you think Jesus felt about this?
3. Share with your group a situation in your life like Sophie's when no time seemed like the right time to reveal the news.

Chapter 3
Let Love Cover

1. How important were those four people in Sophie's life who believed that this was what Jesus was asking of her? Who in your life are you certain would stand beside you in your obedience to Jesus, no matter what?
2. Can you name a time when you were in a communal setting and Jesus touched you in such an intimate way that it felt like the entire service was for you?
3. Is there a place in your life where someone needs to rip up a dollar and tell you, "Money doesn't matter. Jesus matters." Why do you think we battle fear regarding money more than almost anything else?

Chapter 4
Flight 254

1. Have you ever said a yes to Jesus that felt weak and frail but was actually one of the greatest leaps of faith you've ever taken? Discuss those moments with your group, and share the testimony of what Jesus did with your weak and frail yes.
2. Is it sometimes hard to see God's faithfulness? Discuss with the group ways to help each other keep perspective on His unchanging faithfulness even when times are hard.
3. What about this chapter is the most touching to you? How do you feel God is encouraging you at this point in Sophie's story?

Chapter 5
My Brokenness Before Me

1. Have you ever experienced grief so deep that it launched you into a downward spiral where, rather than walking through it, you avoided it? Where did this land you?

2. Where does the first commandment fall in your life? Look long and take time to answer. What areas of your life compete with loving Jesus first? Ask God to cause you to turn and to love Him wholeheartedly.

3. What governs your walk with Jesus? Is it your feelings? Your circumstances? Your personality? Your schedule? Your dreams? Or is it His Word and the Spirit that He has deposited in you? Again, take time to answer.

4. Do you tend to despise your brokenness? How does this chapter minister to your heart? Have you ever considered whether your brokenness could be a launching place into poverty of spirit (seeing your deep and undeniable need for Jesus) and a catapult into the arms of Jesus, who wants to bring you to life with His love?

Chapter 6
You Say My Love Is Real

1. Sophie began to understand that there is love to be found in every place of brokenness. How does this truth manifest itself to you today?

2. She writes, "My emotions were raw and unsanctified, unplanned and authentic, but I wasn't scared. I began to feel a sense of being safe with Him, not concerned that I needed to hide or to tame my bloodied being." Have you experienced moments with Jesus like this? If not, is something causing you to believe that your brokenness must be hidden?

3. John 17 tells us that Jesus desires two things: for us to be with Him where He is and to behold His glory. Meditate on the truth that Jesus desires you to be with Him and to see His glory. Make room for the Spirit to baptize you in His desire.

Chapter 7
Remove All That Hinders

1. What does your relationship with Jesus look like when people close to you are suffering in awful circumstances? What happens in your dialogue with Jesus when nothing you do is visibly changing the situation of the one who is suffering?

2. Sophie talks about learning that she can be one who labors with Jesus. Where is your heart as you recognize that this is the inheritance of all believers and truly reflects God's heart? (Read Romans 8:17.)

3. Are circumstances in your life (past or present) hindering your love for God? Have you become offended through confusion or tragedy, keeping you from being who Jesus made you to be?

4. Sophie writes, "His rod and His staff tenderly met me in the place of confusion and helplessness and, without disregarding my struggle, led me into His gracious presence." How does this minister to you? Do you ever feel like God's promises disregard your struggle? Where do you need grace to allow Him to correct lies and hindrances in your heart toward Him?

Chapter 8
Learning Travail

1. Have you ever experienced travailing prayer? Contemplate the word that Jesus spoke to Sophie about picking up offense or travail.

2. Is there an area of your life in which you have given up fighting for beauty? How does this chapter encourage you to see beauty in the darkest places of your life? Where is beauty waiting to surface in your life? Take time answering and praying through this.

Chapter 9
Called a Satanist

1. When did you first say yes to Jesus? Share this testimony with your group. If you have never said yes to Jesus, today is the day!

2. Is Christianity synonymous with the quest to become a better person? Discuss how this misconception can be incredibly dangerous, and the fine line between pursuing holiness in the Lord, and pursuing mere morality outside of the Gospel.

3. What false accusations have been made against you? Are you walking in freedom, letting Jesus lovingly wrap His promises around you, or are you bound?

Chapter 10
The Sacred In-Between

1. What is a place in your life where you face the in-between? Does it feel impossible to embrace? Encourage one another to press on, knowing intimacy with Jesus is right there.

2. Does the passage from Joel 2 offer encouragement and motivation in your in-between place? Have you ever contemplated the jealousy of our God and His deep compassion for His people?

3. Take a few moments to sit in the jealousy of God. Pray together and ask for His heart.

Chapter 11
Sought After

1. Have you ever tried to cover up deep confusion with a false, comforting theology? Have you ever believed the lie that everything happens for a reason, even convincing yourself that it is scriptural? How does this chapter of Sophie's story encourage you?

2. What are areas of confusion in your life that call for you to acknowledge your lack of understanding? Take time to engage with Jesus about these areas.

3. Have you ever taken time to consider Jesus's pursuit of your heart? His longing for communion with you, as with Adam and Eve in the garden of Eden? Take time to pray with your group about returning to intimacy with Jesus, giving Him what He so greatly desires.

Chapter 12
African Freedom Day

1. What about this story breaks your heart? How do you feel Jesus is speaking to you?
2. What part is Jesus calling you to play in guaranteeing justice for the poor? Have you acted upon that call?

Chapter 13
Songs of Deliverance

1. Has the Enemy ever had you on lockdown? What do you think is the greatest contributor to your shame?
2. Many people get nervous when any discussion of demons or demonic strongholds comes up. Take a few minutes with your group to look through the Gospels (Matthew, Mark, Luke, and John) and to discuss what is recorded in Scripture.

Chapter 14
Healed in His Presence

1. Do you have a testimony of God's healing power in your life or in the life of someone close to you? Share this with the group.
2. In a world filled with so much sin and darkness, it is sometimes difficult to remember all the miracles God has done. How well do you remember the testimonies of His faithfulness to you? Why is it often much easier to remember all the sorrows? Take a few minutes to ask the Lord to restore you to a place of gratitude.
3. Where in your life do you need God's healing power? Are you seeking healing more than you are seeking Him? What are some ways that you can remind yourself of His goodness and bind yourself to His ability?

Chapter 15
She Will Be Called a Mighty Oak

1. How does Sophie's testimony of her first adoption encourage you?
2. Are you a parent? Do you have words from the Lord that you speak over your children daily?
3. Has there been a season in your life when you have felt grace to believe for the impossible? Is it normal for you to have an appetite for the impossible? If not, why not? Pray as a group that your hearts will grow in abandon to Jesus and that He will increase your desire for the impossible.

Chapter 16
Compassion Leads to Miracles

1. How would you define compassion? Have you encountered Jesus's compassion for you? Sophie writes, "Jesus dove into the core of me and planted Himself there. He saw the depths of my depravity and anchored Himself to my plight. My need for compassion could never outsource Him." Discuss this with your group and pray that you might grow in revelation of the Lord's compassion.
2. So often we turn inward and buckle in shame rather than linger in hope before the Lord. Do you agree with Sophie that shame can sometimes feel safe? Discuss a time when you've clung to shame because it felt safer than hope.
3. Discuss the difference between expectant faith and entitlement, and consider how easy it is to slip into entitlement. Spend time inviting the Holy Spirit to speak and to reveal things in your heart to which you may be holding God hostage.
4. How do you respond when you face deep injustices? Are you tempted to believe that God's compassion is absent when injustice prevails?

Chapter 17
A Carrier of Stories

1. Has prayer ever felt like an obituary? Discuss with the group times when praying hasn't felt like enough. Why do you think it is so hard for us simply to pray?

2. The sudden disappearance of Niza is unsettling and disheartening, not the most encouraging or victorious part of Sophie's journey. How does this story leave you hanging? Pay attention to what emotions are rising in your spirit and discuss this as a group. Invite the Holy Spirit to come and to move in you.

3. Sophie says Jesus taught her that the most courageous thing she can do is carry the stories of the brokenhearted and do the work of intimacy with Him. Share with the group your response to this, and pray together that the Lord will increase your capacity to carry stories.

4. What is Jesus speaking to your heart now? At the conclusion of *Crowns of Beauty*, where is your heart moved? Share, pray, and press on into Jesus's presence.

5. How has this book changed your perspective on missionary life? Have you ever considered the pressures that missionaries face to continually share victorious testimonies with churches and supporters? What changes must be made within the church so that missionaries can be authentic about what is happening on the ground?

6. This final chapter depicts a victory far greater than circumstance. Take time to meditate on this, and be launched into Jesus Himself.

Made in the USA
Lexington, KY
29 November 2017